Taming the
Terrible Too's
of Training

How to improve workplace performance in the digital age

Amanda:

Best wishes!

Ken Cooper
March 2015

Taming the
Terrible Too's
of Training

How to improve workplace performance in the digital age

Dan Cooper and Ken Cooper

TotalComm Press

St. Louis

Taming the Terrible Too's of Training: How to improve workplace
performance in the digital age
Dan Cooper and Ken Cooper

This publication is designed to provide accurate and authoritative information in
regard to the subject matter covered. It is sold with the understanding that the publisher
is not engaged in rendering legal, accounting, or other professional service. If legal
advice or other expert assistance is required, the services of a competent professional
person should be sought.

ISBN-13: 978-0-9850949-3-5
ISBN-10/ASIN: 0-9850949-3-1

No Push Selling® is a registered trademark of CooperComm, Inc. A.I.M.® is a registered
trademark of AIM Consulting. All other names, companies, brands, products, and
services mentioned in this book are the trade names or registered trademarks of their
respective owners.

The editor of this book was Joan Reinbott, and the designer was Peggy Nehmen.
This book is set in Melior Medium and Gotham Bold.

First Printing

For Ali, Owen, Josie, and Ben.
D.C.

For Sue, who has been so patient with this
wild ride called a training career.
K.C.

Contents

Preface

THIS BOOK IS A PRACTICAL ROADMAP for creating employee training that actually works in this digital age. It is a mix of both theory and practice, developed from experience in training for thousands of organizations and from analyzing extensive academic and industry research.

Our goal is to show how to use training to "move the needle" on your business results in the most time-efficient and cost-effective way possible. To accomplish that, we do several things here:

1. Identify dysfunctional training processes that are common in organizations today.
2. Address the "disconnect" between current employee training practices and the realities of adult learning in today's work environment.
3. Share research on instructional design that shows exactly how to maximize learning, retention, and transfer of knowledge to the workplace.
4. Identify a new role for the Training department in a digital age learning environment.

The approach we have identified is called "right" learning—workplace training that *features the right need, right time, right amount, and right design.*

The "we" in this book represents the collective voice of the authors. Between us, we have over 50 combined years in the training industry.

We have presented over 2,500 in-person training seminars, have appeared in hundreds of live satellite TV broadcasts, and have developed in excess of 1,000 online training programs. We have completed the transition from classroom training to nearly total e-learning delivery using online video. Along the way, we have had experience with early computer-based training tools and now we deliver e-learning over the Web to all "six screens"—smartphones, tablets, PCs, portable media players, route handhelds, and TVs.

This book's structure is consistent with the research on adult learning that it champions. We have organized the content into short chapters, each one dealing with a single learning point. The flow of the book is from fundamentals to details, as effective instructional design requires. Specific action steps are provided at the end of each chapter to help you move the needle on your training results.

Here is what we cover:

Part 1 introduces the current issues with workplace training, what we call the "Terrible Too's."

Part 2 discusses the overall value of training. It addresses the two most frequent questions concerning training.

Part 3 consolidates the relevant research on adult learning and applies it to workplace training.

Part 4 covers practical research in instructional design for workplace training.

Part 5 examines training deployment and delivery and evaluates the pros and cons of various media.

Part 6 explains how to create an effective training strategy.

Part 7 takes a big picture look at the future of training and explores the Training department's potential new role at the center of an enterprise-wide unified communications architecture.

A reference section is included at the back of the book so that you can see the original sources for research that we footnote.

Throughout the text, for clarity we capitalize the word "Training" when it refers to the Training department itself. We use lowercase "training" when it refers to the general function of training or the actual learning activities.

As a training professional, you know that knowledge without action is just noise. That is why each chapter has a "To Do" section detailing how you can use the information in this book to move the scorecard needle on *your* training results.

Dan Cooper
Ken Cooper
August 2012

Acknowledgments

ACKNOWLEDGMENTS AND THANKS GO TO:

Anita Marx, A.I.M. consultant and Baldrige Examiner extraordinaire, who makes sure we understand what excellence really is.

Bob Stuckey and Larry Heidemann, who sat at the big table and know what it takes to truly make a difference.

All the great clients from wonderful companies, who made the decision to implement "right" learning and taught us so much in return.

Part 1

Training in the Digital Age

THE HARVARD BUSINESS SCHOOL conducted a survey of nearly 10,000 of its alumni concerning U.S. competitiveness.[1] The report included a tally of suggestions for government officials plus actions that companies might take to help their U.S. operations compete more effectively.

Within the *Suggestions for Government Officials:*

- Only 112 of 4,425 responses were "Invest in education and training in general."
- In contrast, "Reform immigration policies" was suggested 322 times.

These leaders were evidently more concerned with increasing the availability of qualified foreign workers than they were with improving the training of their current employees.

In addition, within the *Actions for Firms:*

- Only 128 of 1,747 responses were "Invest more in training and developing employees."
- In contrast, "Hire more skilled labor/improve recruiting" was indicated 141 times.

From this, leaders seem to be more concerned with becoming better at hiring needed talent rather than developing it.

These are just two more points in a long line of data indicating the lack of confidence organizational leadership has in training. It can no longer be ignored. Something is wrong with workplace learning in the digital age. The important questions are:

What is wrong with training?
Why is there a disconnect?
What is the challenge for the Training department?

1.1

The "Terrible Too's" of Training

EMPLOYEE TRAINING IS BIG BUSINESS. Organizations spend $52.8 billion annually on outside training, including payroll and external products and services.[1] The e-learning portion makes up $18.2 billion of that amount and is expected to increase to $24.2 billion by 2015.[2] So there is no question that organizations are making significant investments in employee development.

Conceptually, there is universal agreement that training is an important factor in the overall success of organizations. Everyone believes that employees need to be taught how to do their jobs properly. But practically, there is a long-standing question among leaders as to whether or not the training function is justified from a payback standpoint.

A startling observation in *Transfer of Learning* back in 2000 addressed the historical value of training: "Most of the research on employee training clearly shows that, although millions of dollars are spent on training, there is little empirical evidence linking training to improved job behavior or employee attitudes."[3] In contrast, other research has suggested that education and training is a significant predictor of an organization's success as measured by price-to-earnings ratios, price-to-book statistics, and measures of risk and volatility.[4]

So which is it for training, bane or boon?

The reality is that organizations really haven't known what payoff training was providing. A survey published in *Training Magazine* reported that only about 3% of organizations were using Kirkpatrick's Level 4 (business results) measures.[5]

In the intervening years, the situation doesn't appear to have changed much. Although overall training expenditures are holding relatively steady, per-employee spending on training is declining.[6] And the effectiveness of employee training is still in question. There continues to be almost nothing in the literature regarding the actual direct payback of learning initiatives. As a result, training is often the first thing to be cut in a tough economy. So what is going on?

> *There is a giant disconnect between how organizations provide training and the realities of adult learning.*

Over the past 70 years, academic researchers have studied just about every imaginable factor in adult education for both classroom and e-learning. Yet the typical trainer has no idea what this research is or how to adjust the organization's training programs accordingly. As a result, most workplace learning activities suffer from what we call the "Terrible Too's" of training. These are:

Too disconnected. Training exists by itself on a departmental island. There is little connection between the overall organizational initiatives and the courses being offered.

Too much. Learners can only absorb so much information and have only so much brainpower to process it. But because it is so costly to take workers off the job, organizations commonly create brain dump events to tell attendees everything at once. The reality of adult learning is that if you overload human memory, people don't retain a portion of the content. They remember none of it.

Too long. Learners have limited attention spans, which research says is in the 10-minute range. This is due to an individual's inherent ability to concentrate, as well as the steady stream of interruptions throughout the work day. It's a fantasy to think that learners can maintain full attention throughout an 8-hour class or a 90-minute webcast. They physically can't do it, and the workplace environment wouldn't let them even if they could.

Too early. Most employee training is "anticipation learning" (i.e., training delivered well in advance of the on-the-job application of those new skills). The longer the delay, the less effective the training is.

Too infrequent. Organizational learning is usually offered as a single event. Considering the realities of adult retention, it's another fantasy to assume that the attendees retain more than a shred of content over the intervening months and years, especially without reinforcement. And what about employees hired after that training event? They get no exposure to the content whatsoever. So without a refresh learning process in operation, there is little to no learning taking place over time.

Too boring. It's not enough that most training is too much, too long, and too early. The icing on the cake is that it is often too boring. We're all professional TV watchers. We've been conditioned to expect visually stimulating content. We'll gladly play along at home with long-time classics such as *Jeopardy!* or *Wheel of Fortune*. But we have no tolerance for "death by *PowerPoint*" presentations or for click-and-read e-learning where stilted text is read to us word for word while we look at verbatim text and static graphics.

Too inconsistent. Consistency is not a problem with e-learning, but it is definitely an issue with classroom training and live webcasts. There are always differences between instructors, and there can even be day-to-day variations with the same instructor. In addition, attendee questions are usually different, which can lead programs into unexpected directions. As a result of all this, both the quality of instruction and the content itself can vary widely across different audiences.

Too inconvenient. Most training requires employees to leave their workplace, or at least temporarily abandon their work for an extended period. This lost time goes beyond the event itself because of the time spent traveling and getting back into the flow of work. Certainly, white collar workers can complete e-learning programs on their laptop or desktop PC, but this is not the case for other employees. Then when attendees return to the job, they are essentially punished for leaving because of the backlog of calls, e-mails, and stacked-up work.

Too expensive. Traditional training is a costly proposition and is much more expensive than many organizations realize. It requires a lot of money to bring people together, whether it is in a room or online. In addition to the direct costs of the training itself, there are often hidden and indirect expenses, such as travel costs or opportunity costs. It's no wonder that managers are always looking for ways to cut the training budget.

Too dysfunctional. The entire training process is often completely dysfunctional:
- Training is viewed as simply a completion event, where the main goal is to establish an active defense against lawsuits.
- No one talks to the learners to find out what they actually need to improve their performance.
- Training is not really training. It is a one-way information dump.
- Trainers buy authoring tools because they are easy to use, not because they generate compelling content.
- Management is told that there is a complete online curriculum available, but it consists entirely of horribly boring programs that no one takes.
- Employees are not given sufficient time-to-do to actually practice and master new skills.
- There is no refresh learning process to keep new skills top of mind.
- Managers are not in the loop, so they cannot coach to the new skills.
- There is negative feedback during the learning curve with new skills, so employees stop attempting them.

The list can go on and on.

Does any of this sound familiar? It's no wonder that employees run away from training like they are being chased by zombies and that managers pick up a red pencil before they even look at a training budget.

That brings us to *Taming the Terrible Too's*. A rational training process does exist. Solid research shows how to create training that engages learners and truly improves performance on the job. Specific methods for developing and deploying training can dramatically lower costs, both for today and in the future.

Some organizations "get" learning. For them, training is indeed moving the needle on their scorecard measures, and they are tangibly improving their business results. But they are not doing it the old, traditional way. Instead of ignoring the realities of adult learning in the digital age, they are taking advantage of them. What follows is exactly how they are doing it.

○ To Do

This one is simple.

1. Continue reading.

Fact or Myth? How Good Is Your Research?

THIS BOOK IS ALL ABOUT FACTS, surprising as they are. We are not providing opinions. We're taking the extensive amount of educational research available today and following it to its inescapable conclusions. That is the reason for the extensive Reference section at the end of the book.

You need to use the same approach in your training. The key question is, "Are you making training decisions for the right reasons?" The answer is, maybe not.

In doing research on the effectiveness of various e-learning media, we ran across some useful research that is commonly quoted across the Internet:

- According to Albert Mehrabian, 55% of what we communicate is through body language, 38% is through tone of voice, and 7% is through words.
- As illustrated in The Learning Pyramid, after two weeks people tend to remember 10% of what they read, 20% of what they hear, 30% of what they see, 50% of what they hear and see, 70% of what they say, and 90% of what they say and do.
- Researchers at Simon Fraser University found that the average continuous attention span for literate humans is 8 seconds with a maximum of 30 seconds, and the average general attention span is from 10 to 12 minutes.

This is all critical information for anyone trying to figure out what type of e-learning media to use, and how long to make courses. Right?

GOTCHA! *All of these research statistics are MYTHS.* They are simply not true. So what in the world is going on?

First, many people still seem to accept whatever they find on the Internet as fact. Just look at all the weird stuff friends e-mail you. It takes a dedicated site like Snopes.com just to keep up with all the falsehoods making the rounds online.

Second, although everyone knows how to do online searches, no one is training people on how to evaluate what they find. People don't check the credentials of online authors, and they don't question the accuracy of the content.

Third, many people don't do any further checking to see if there are contrasting opinions or research.[1]

It's different in academia. Authors there must go through a peer review process to weed out the pretenders from the pros and fiction from the facts. Researchers are required to reference the original source for any research they quote.

There is no such refereed journal process on the Internet, where it is the Wild West of information. When it comes to online references, people quote people who quote people … who quote the first person. This is what's called a *circular attribution*, where a so-called fact takes on a life of its own without any identifiable origin.

Or sometimes it's an online version of the whisper game, where a message slowly gets warped over time as it passes from expert to author to e-zine columnist to blogger to business user. They may all intend to accurately quote each other, but a steady stream of mistakes creeps in.

If you do your homework, here is what you discover about our examples:

The first myth is a misquote of Mehrabian's classic work in nonverbal communication.[2] He studied how people show whether or not they *like* one another, and he wanted to determine the relative contribution of facial expression, tone of voice, and words to "liking." That is what the 55, 38, and 7 numbers refer to, *not* to the contribution of each in general communication.

As for the second myth, search on "learning pyramid hoax," and you'll find that the source everyone references, National Training Laboratory, has no actual data to support the Pyramid, and that it's derived from Edgar Dale's Cone of Experience dating back to the 1940s.[3] Do further research on Dale's work and you'll learn that his Cone model was never intended as anything more than a conceptual metaphor, and that Dale warned readers not to take it too literally.

The third myth is simply a big question mark. Although an online search returns a number of references to the attention study, no original paper can be found. And when we called the Psychology, Communication, and Education departments at Simon Fraser University in Canada, they had never heard of the research.

As the Mythbusters on TV say, "Mark these FALSE."

○ To Do

How can you be certain you are using valid research? Unfortunately, there is no academic equivalent of Snopes.com to help with the vast amount of training-related information strewn across the Internet. It is up to you to follow these simple guidelines:

1. Start with a skeptical attitude. Just because you can find something in a Google search or on Wikipedia does not mean it's for real. Paranoia is good.
2. Apply a sniff test to Web authors. Check their credentials, if stated, to see if you have a qualified expert or an opinionated amateur.
3. Look for bias. Be alert to the writing style of a site to see if someone has an academic interest or is pushing a personal agenda.
4. Use a similar sniff test for what you read. All three myths mentioned previously should have made your nose wrinkle right from the start. Think about it:
   - Only 7% of what we communicate overall is by words? That makes no sense whatsoever. Words are obviously the primary medium of communication, not the least important. Otherwise, we would spend most of our day grunting and

gesturing at each other, and phone and e-mail would be virtually useless.

- Learning Pyramid percentages increase by exact 10s? You know human behavior variables are not that consistent. What valid research could possibly result in round tens and equal increments? It's not credible.

- Average attention span for a literate human is 8 seconds with a maximum of 30 seconds? With that attention span, how did the human get to be literate in the first place? And what's with this weird "literate human" terminology, and where did that come from? It's not a commonly used research term.

You can sniff these out immediately.

5. Dig beyond secondary references to find the original source documents. If the data is important, a publication will be out there somewhere.

6. Actually review the original research you find. True, most of it is not exactly fireside reading. But you need to understand any assumptions behind the research to see if it is applicable to your situation. That means you have to dig into it.

7. Look for opposing opinions, which is common in academia. Just because someone quotes a fact doesn't mean that no other research refutes it. Ideas evolve. And when theories are in dispute, researchers love to debate point-counterpoint throughout a long series of publications. Make sure you get both sides of the discussion.

8. When in doubt, ask an expert. There is probably an education department at a nearby college. Check with the teaching professionals there. That's exactly what we did in researching this chapter.

Suppose you see an article in the *New York Times* quoting research that workers average only eleven and one-half minutes between interruptions. This is an important figure to know if you are trying to determine how long an e-learning course should be. But is it valid?

Do your homework and you will find the 2005 paper, "No Task Left Behind? Examining the Nature of Fragmented Work," from researchers at the School of Information and Computer Science of University of California, Irvine.[4] You read it and see that it involved white-collar workers. Mark this one TRUE.

Treat Training as a Profession

THE FINAL BIG-PICTURE ISSUE we need to consider before digging into the Terrible Too's involves the organizational attitude toward training. How is it possible that the Terrible Too's exist, that Training departments are making decisions for the wrong reasons, or that the information in this book comes as such a surprise to many trainers?

An internationally known author on workplace learning tells the story of addressing about 200 training professionals. In his talk, he made a casual reference to Kirkpatrick's third level of training evaluation. He saw some blank looks, so he asked how many of the attendees were familiar with the Kirkpatrick model. Only about one-third of the attendees raised their hands.[1]

He points out with dismay that this is a fundamental concept in organizational learning. Imagine if two-thirds of your auditors did not know what a Chart of Accounts is, or if two-thirds of your salespeople didn't know how to handle objections, or if two-thirds of your information technology people didn't know how to back up a hard disk. What would that suggest about how well things are running at your place? Well, it's no different for Training.

The unfortunate reality is, in most organizations, training is not treated as a profession. In fact, it is often staffed with individuals poorly qualified for the job. As a result, it's not getting the respect that it deserves, and it's not getting the results required of it. And this starts right at the top.

Look at the leaders within your organization. The CEO has an MBA. The head of Legal is an attorney. The head of Accounting is a CPA. The head of Research and Development is a Ph.D. The head of Engineering is a P.E. They have all met educational and/or professional standards for their respective vocations. And in many cases, these certifications require them to keep updating their knowledge and skills with continuing education.

Now take a look at who is running the Training department. Is it a top leader who is experienced in adult learning principles and education administration? Probably not. Only 8% of Fortune 1000 companies have a C-level executive directly responsible for training, and that number is growing by only 2% per year.[2]

Or is Training being headed up by a spare manager who has led various departments and was available? Training isn't going to get respect at the executive big table until its leader has status and domain expertise equal to everyone else there.

Next, look at the Training staff. Is the department full of experienced educators? Are they up to date on the current instructional design research? Do they know how to use the latest educational technologies? Do they understand the learning consulting process? Learning project management? Instructional design? Course writing and delivery? Or are they novices from other departments rotated through Training for two-year terms on their way to their first management position?

If you can get a degree in something, then it's a profession. Colleges offer majors in education and instructional design. Therefore, training is a profession. If you are getting treated like amateurs, then maybe it's because some of your people are amateurs, or are perceived as amateurs.

◑ To Do

Audit your Training department to determine who is actually qualified to be in their positions. For those who aren't qualified:

1. Lobby decision makers to provide leaders who have expertise in workplace learning. This doesn't require an ivory tower educator. This means Training leaders should have the education, the

learning experience, and the industry acumen to produce effective training that tangibly benefits the organization.

2. Lobby those leaders to staff the Training department with experts qualified in the various facets of employee learning. Help them understand that these jobs are not simply tour stops for upwardly mobile generic management trainees. Executives wouldn't rotate a non-accountant through the tax department. There's too much at risk. The same is true of Training. The productivity of the entire employee base is at stake.

3. If you have to take whoever gets assigned to you, then do what you do best. Turn these novices into learning experts with your own Training 101 curriculum. That means giving this effort the full meal deal—creating standards, providing training and learning resources, tracking progress and achievement, and coaching performance. Depending upon your budget, resources can include:

   • One-on-one coaching and mentoring.
   • Reading lists. (The Reference section in this book provides a large list of books, periodicals, e-newsletters, online research, and bloggers covering training.)
   • Internal training programs on topics such as instructional design, program authoring, and presentation skills.
   • Benchmarking of local firms.
   • e-Learning courses and webcasts.
   • Vendor training on products and courseware development tools.
   • Local college courses.
   • Industry conferences.

4. Provide continuing education for the department. This can include periodic meetings to update everyone on recent research. It could be circulating publications and online articles. It could be conducting and sharing periodic searches on key training topics. It could be going through this book one chapter at a time.

You will know you've accomplished your goal of creating a professional training organization when you no longer have to beg other departments to come to you with their training needs. Your constituents will seek you out. Why? Because you are the recognized experts in training people and improving performance.

Part 2

Establishing the
Value of Training

WE'RE STILL MAD ABOUT all the time we wasted in Chemistry 101 worrying about a "mole" of something (the number of particles in 12 grams of carbon 12). We learned how to convert moles to grams and back again, and to calculate equivalent moles of one thing to another. We still don't know why. We've never since used the information. You can't buy a mole of gasoline, or a mole of bread, or a mole of lumber. You don't do your taxes in moles. As a measurement, the mole seems to have no use in the real world.

How much of what you learn, or for that matter what you are teaching, is a "mole" of content that has little recognized value in the organization? How can you instead make sure you are providing training that literally justifies your very existence? It requires answering these questions:

Who are the three customers of training?
What value does training provide to each of them?
What is the required payoff for training?
What does it take to generate that payoff?

Who Are the Customers of Training?

SEVERAL YEARS AGO we attended a meeting of the wholesaler training group at a big brewer. A great thing about this company was that it had a single-minded focus. No matter what the meeting was about, someone was bound to ask, "How does this help us sell more beer?" This time was no different.

The event was a multi-day planning and education session for the entire Training department along with its repertory company of about 30 outside trainers and learning consultants. At that time, Training reported up through sales, with the company recognizing that a skilled distributor team was essential to maintaining and growing its market share.

There was a Training Update presentation early in the agenda, with two high-level sales executives attending for just that session. The Update contained all the usual information: total courses available, topics and titles covered, number of programs taught both in person and online, total student-days and student-hours delivered, new course development, technology performance and plans, budgets, and projections for the next year. The executives listened quietly through it all, but you could see their impatient body language.

Finally, one of the VPs asked, "OK, I get all that. But what about results?"

The Training director went back to his summary information, "As you saw, we delivered X,000 student days, we had X,000 online logins, we delivered XXX programs …" In the middle of this he was cut off by the increasingly irritated executive.

"No," the VP said, "what are the *results*? What have you accomplished?" But the director didn't get it. He kept on quoting Training department performance numbers. This went on for a bit, until the exasperated VP said, "Fine" and ended the discussion.

The Training department employees didn't seem fazed by the exchange, but we consultants were all looking at each other in alarm. There was an obvious problem here, potentially affecting funding for our services. Then both VPs were gone at the next break.

Speaking of gone, it was just a few months after the meeting that the director was gone, too, sent into an early retirement. He just didn't understand what his bosses wanted from the Training department.

The question is, "Who are the customers of Training?" A number of possibilities exist:

Internal. This is the manufacturing model of training, where the department is like a factory producing events. The main goal is to keep the training production line moving. Success is measured just like the Update above—on departmental activity.

Learners. This is the school model of training. Here the focus is on the individual learners, essentially separate from the organization as a whole. The goal is to return attendees to their workplace with new knowledge and skills. What happens before or after that is not a function of Training. The classic measure of this approach is comparing the gain from pre- to post-tests.

Other departments. This is the external model of training. Some Training groups exist to serve other departments. Human Resources (HR), Legal, and Safety require compliance training and record keeping for certification. Finance needs everything to be charged to the right account. Information technology (IT) needs support for learning management systems and e-learning delivery. As long as all these other groups aren't complaining, no one is going to look too closely at what's actually happening in Training.

"The system." This is the institutional model of training, where the focus is on doing the same things year after year. Here training activities take on a life of their own through sheer momentum. Major programs have evolved into classics that have been in place for decades. New managers go to new manager school. Employees have locked-in position curricula. There is always the annual sales reward seminar ... and on and on. The measure of success is simply completing the same training agenda each year.

We're not saying that these are all unworthy candidates for Training's customers. Training itself needs to be a smooth running machine internally. Skilled learners are definitely a necessary output of effective training. The Training department has to co-exist with other departments. And Training has to complete its assignments. But none of these so-called "customers" can keep the spigot flowing when it comes to funding. So it's unavoidable:

> *The primary customers of Training are the executives who provide funding for the department. They have needles to move.*

Training lives in a far more competitive environment than it realizes. Although executives give lip service to the importance of employee training, it's not considered to be in the same class as sales, marketing, finance, legal, administration, or operations. Executives can't completely eliminate these functions and still keep operating. But they can eliminate training, and they may not notice any difference when they do.

Another important customer set is typically ignored by Training.

> *The customers of Training are also the managers who are responsible for improving the performance of their employees when they return from training.*

Certainly there are training programs for the managers themselves, including a generic coaching process. That's not what we are saying. We're talking about whether or not the training process formally involves the managers of learners. Usually, they have no structured role in training. Their people take classes and return afterwards. Then everyone goes back to work as if the training never happened.

You can guarantee that if managers do not know what is being taught, then they certainly can't be coaching to it. And if managers are not tolerant of trial-and-error mistakes during the learning curve for new skills, then learners will quickly understand that there is no benefit to changing. So the result is, without a manager's formal involvement and support, training is a complete waste of time.

So it's essential to understand that there are actually three customers of Training: leaders, managers, and learners. The focus is sometimes on none of them, and often on only one of them (learners). Expanding your definition for customers of Training can help improve results and keep the budget money flowing.

▷ To Do

Expand the perspective of your Training department.

1. Make a strong cultural statement concerning satisfying your customers.
2. Make sure everyone understands who your customers are: the executives who fund the department, the managers who are responsible for employee performance before and after a training event, and the learners themselves.
3. Find out what their respective scorecard needles are.

Keep your executives happy and you will never have budget struggles. Help them to move their needles and you'll get more funding than you ever dreamed possible. Keep the remaining two customers happy, and you won't have to fight to get people to attend your training.

2.2

How Do You Get Leadership to Value Training?

IT WAS ONE OF THOSE SURREAL MOMENTS where we didn't know what to say next. We were chatting with the CEO of a very successful consulting firm. His company's Home page highlighted their well-trained workforce as one of the key reasons to use their services. Naturally we were curious and asked, "So how do you train your consultants?"

He replied, "Actually, we don't have any training specifically for consultants. We have a subscription to some generic online learning courses, but no one takes them."

"Oh," we managed, and moved on to another topic.

Here is an organization promoting its commitment to training, but it doesn't actually provide any. In other organizations, we have seen executives similarly extolling their commitment to improving the skills of employees even as they were slashing the training budget. Like it or not, there is often this major contradiction between how training is spoken about versus how training is actually supported.

So what do your leaders think of your Training department?

Do they understand the function?

Do they have confidence in your staff?

Do they think of Training as a strategic partner?

Do they feel Training is significant enough to sit at the big table?

Do they view Training as a resource to be leveraged versus an expense to be managed?

Do they call the Training department when they are under pressure to move a needle?

Sadly, for most organizations the answer to all these questions is, "No." If leaders can slash training costs, they will and not think twice about it.

After a few years of watching budgets shrink, training professionals develop a Rodney Dangerfield complex, "We don't get no respect." In fact, put a bunch of trainers together with an outside expert and you'll invariably hear Classic Question #1:

"How do I get management to value training?"

The common answer is the usual list of platitudes:
• Become a strategic partner.
• Promote the role of training in organizational productivity improvement.
• Do a better job of marketing training courses.
• Listen to the needs of client departments.
• Upgrade your methods of delivery.
• Seek additional training opportunities, whether inside or outside the organization.
• Change the way you measure success.

This is all good advice, but it's dancing around the problem. The real issue is that Training is acting like an academic institution while executives are running a business.

Organizational leaders have to find ways to make money or, in the case of non-profits, to not lose money. These executives think in terms of strategy, competition, products and services, initiatives, and cash flow. They have scorecard measures to manage (i.e., needles to move and bonuses to earn). This terminology is alien to the training department, which is focused on schedules, courses, attendees, test scores, smile sheets, and record keeping.

The reality for Training is that you simply *must* contribute to the bottom line. Ideally, a Training department should not even need funding.

The best training group we have ever seen was a zero-budget operation. It was tasked with training a company's field sales force and its dealer channel consisting of independently owned small businesses. This training group could do anything it wanted as long as it could find someone to pay for it. Field sales training was funded out of the sales budget, and the distributor owners paid for it out of their own pocket.

It was a true survival-of-the-fittest environment. The Training department either delivered value in excess of its costs or it was out of business. The parent company didn't care either way. Training was always available from somewhere else. Yet this department grew year after year. So how do you generate similar success?

▷ **To Do**

Here is what it takes to get executive leadership to value training:

1. Regardless of how you are actually funded, act like a profit center. Focus on the hard dollar return your department generates, and work to document it. Move a scorecard needle. (There is more on this in a coming chapter.)

2. Understand that all the headache stuff you have to do will keep you from getting fired, but it won't make your executives love you. By headache stuff, we mean the required content such as hiring and firing, sexual harassment, Health Insurance Portability and Accountability Act (HIPAA), safety, i.e., all the nuts and bolts of employee training. About all you can do for these is to make sure that your executives know about it whenever a competitor or neighbor gets sued.

3. Sit down with key decision makers and have a candid conversation about how they view Training. Find out what they think about the value currently being delivered by your department. They will all have an opinion, and they'll appreciate you for initiating the conversation. Take your lumps if you have to, and don't be defensive. They are helping you create a roadmap for success.

4. Become more strategic. Find out what needles executives want moved. Develop a maniacal focus on your organization's key

initiatives, and explicitly support them. This is the short list of items that are the focus points for the year, such as this sample from one organization:

- Grow revenue
- Back to basics on service
- Leverage Six Sigma

It would be a simple exercise for this organization's Training department to go through its entire course catalog and identify which offerings *specifically* address these initiatives. Generic training such as Key Account Selling doesn't count for the revenue item. It takes titles such as, "How to sell more units to existing customers" or "How to win against Competitor A."

For many departments, this one exercise can be a sobering wake-up call when they see how few (if any) of their offerings directly contribute to key strategic initiatives. It's no wonder their executives don't see any value in training. If this is the case in your department, then you know where to focus your development efforts.

5. Become more tactical. Establish Training as the go-to source for solutions to pain points other departments are experiencing. Training needs to be a resource rather than a burden that spends money and takes workers off the job. As in #3, this means creating task-oriented training to deal with specific issues.

6. Take your education hat off and put your executive hat on. Look at your department the way the two sales VPs looked at the brewery training group. Then measure your results the way your executives do. It's not about course days and smile sheets. It's about business results in excess of the cost of the training itself.

In the annual initiatives example earlier, although there may not be a true one-to-one cause-and-effect relationship, if the programs are designed properly, there are many possible links that will resonate with executives.

Revenue growth? You could create some great courses:
How to sell high-end units.
How to win against Competitor A.
How to close in fewer calls.
How to sell with smaller discounts.

Back to basics on service? You might create programs like these:
How to answer the Top 10 complaints.
Using service calls to sell.

Leveraging Six Sigma? Measure how much trainees are generating in terms of process improvement efficiencies and reduced errors and rework.

You need to start thinking like the executives who are funding your department. You need to act like you are a zero-budget profit center. Everything you do needs to be justified on how it contributes to the profitability (or non-loss if you are non-profit) of your organization. Then there will never be a question as to the value of your training. Your executives won't be able to live without you.

Training as a Strategic Advantage

IT WAS AN IMPRESSIVE EXAMPLE of out-executing a competitor. The local distributor for a major consumer goods company hired a salesperson away from another company in the market. He started on a Thursday and happened to mention that his former employer was going to roll out a new product to grocery stores for two weeks starting the following Monday. The competitor was offering to buy an end-aisle display and in return wanted the retailer to discount the new product 30 cents below cost. The competitor's message was that the retailer would make up the difference in "market basket add-on" because of the draw of the new product being on special.

The distributor immediately notified the company's national training group of the upcoming competitive campaign. On Friday the trainers came up with a counter-strategy using their own segment-leading product and wrote the training program.

Their recommended pitch for retailers was, "This is a great idea, only it's the wrong product. First, we'll pay you the same amount for the end-aisle display. Second, we suggest you only discount 15 cents, and put the other 15 cents back in your pocket. Third, you'll sell 200 units of their new product off that display, but you'll sell 2,000 units with our leading product and get 10 times the market basket add-on. We can install that display by this weekend, if that's OK."

On Monday the Training group recorded a video program and uploaded it to the online learning site. They recommended that distributors have a Tuesday morning meeting with their salespeople and then call on all their grocery customers that day.

Results? The company was actually making calls countering the rollout before its competitor had even reached most of its retailers. The rollout was stopped in its tracks, and the competitor's product languishes in obscurity to this day.

How did this happen? The competitor spent months planning the rollout and two weeks executing it, whereas the company went from notification to sales execution *in three days!* This company was quicker on its feet than the competitor. It was simply more agile, which is a major advantage in the marketplace.

The Baldrige *Criteria for Performance Excellence* (CPE) lists "agility" as one of the 10 core values found in high-performing organizations. The *CPE* defines agility as "a capacity for rapid change and flexibility." It goes on to observe, "A major success factor in meeting competitive challenges is the design-to-introduction ... or innovation cycle time."[1]

So how does this apply to training in general? Everybody talks about time-to-market of products and services. It is a B-school staple. But there is another angle to agility, as this consumer goods company recognized.

> *Training departments must provide a strategic competitive advantage in the time-to-market of information and skills.*

The classic American Management Association video, *TIME: The Next Dimension of Quality,* calls this "time-based competition." It's the idea that "you've got to make it, market it, and sell it, not just better, but *faster* than your rivals."[2]

Talk about catching the attention of those folks at the big table with the checkbooks. How about your Training department being the engine for derailing a competitor's major product rollout? How about accomplishing in days what it took a competitor months to do, as well as doing it better? Now you're talking strategic value.

The key questions are, "Where is your Training department on the agility scale? Are you an execution engine waiting to be revved up? Are you masters at rapidly addressing training and information requirements? Is your cycle time shorter than your competitors' cycle time? Or are you an elephant graveyard where urgent needs go to die, smothered in surveys, analyses, designer meetings, production team reviews, IT upload delays, and learning management systems intricacies? Are you the guarantee that nothing will happen quickly?"

○ To Do

To make sure you're the solution and not the problem:

1. Make the decision to become an agility engine that your executives can depend on. Set your goal to have the shortest time-to-market of information and skills of anyone in your competitive space.
2. Find out what your constituents think of your current cycle time. You may be surprised by what you hear, and not in a good way.
3. Build a rapid-response capability within your Training department. This isn't a special "rush" scramble. It's the standard rapid deployment process when one is called for. You won't have to use it for all your work, but you'll need it when you get something urgent.
4. Make your overall need-to-solution cycle time a key departmental measure, for both rapid-response projects and normal work. Make cycle time a continuous improvement target.
5. Then create a payoff. Find out about threats early enough to do something to counteract them.

Shortening your cycle time is the gift that keeps on giving because it tends to drag other business measures along with it. As the *CPE* points out, "Time improvements often drive simultaneous improvements in work systems, organization, quality, cost, supply-chain integration, productivity, and sustainability in a challenging economy."[3] These all make Training a better strategic resource for your organization.

2.4

The Payoff Required of Training

TRAINING PROFESSIONALS SEEM TO STRUGGLE when it comes to documenting the hard-dollar benefits of training, but it's much easier for managers on the front lines. One of the best justification analyses we've ever seen involved a regional agriculture vendor.[1]

This company was in dire straits. Its industry was dominated by three giants. Its part-time sales force of farmer-dealers was calling on only 22% of the growers in its territories, and there had been five consecutive years of declining sales. The company was literally in a "last one out turn off the lights" situation.

With no Training department at the company, the VP of sales in the Western Sales Region decided to create an online training series for dealers. It began with 20 programs covering basic sales skills and prospecting. The goal was simple: *get new customers.* It was highly targeted, very tactical training.

The most popular program showed how to get past call-stoppers at the beginning of a sales call, comments such as, "I buy from my brother-in-law" or "I planted your seed last year and it didn't perform." This course was so valuable that viewing logs showed dealers watched it an average of three times, wanting to make sure they had mastered the techniques.

Here were the results of the first buying season after the training:

- New customers went from 565 the previous year to 4,615. (The previous all-time record was 1,650.)
- Sales increased by 22% to a new company high, more than making up for the five years of decline.

- 35% of orders included a high-margin seed treatment add-on versus an industry average of under 4%.

There were also some unexpected benefits:
- It took three fewer calls to close orders.
- Switched or returned orders went from 21%, nearly twice the industry average, to 6.5%, just over half the industry average.
- New dealer sign-ups went from 150 to 370, and existing dealer resignations went from 90 to 30.
- Customer satisfaction improved by one full point on a five-point scale.

What made this particularly powerful was that the Eastern Sales Region chose to not utilize the training. Although there were some other factors in play there, this essentially created a control group situation. Without the training, the Eastern Sales Region remained at 300 new customers and had a seed treatment attach rate of just over 4%. It was no surprise when a few months later the Western Sales Region VP was made national head of sales.

That's the way executives at the big table do it. Training professionals often give lip service to the "return on investment (ROI) of training," but they rarely have anything like this to show for it. And even if they do their justification homework up front, they fail to come back afterwards and document whether or not those goals were achieved, nor do they use their experience to improve future training efforts.

Think of the projects that you have under way. Is there a financial benefit projection for any of them? Think of projects you have recently completed. Is there any analysis comparing the projections with your actual results? If so, and if they're off, do you know why and are you adjusting accordingly in upcoming projects?

It's All About Payback
Even when trainers do their justification homework, they typically use the wrong measures. You'll hear trainers say, "This project generates a 15% ROI over five years." The problem is that leaders aren't interested

in ROI—percentage returns over multiple years. They may be in a different job by then or working at a different organization. So why should they care?

Executives need immediate results. Their bonuses are usually tied to annual performance goals. What they really want is, "Show me where I can spend a dollar today and get more than a dollar back before the end of the budget year." Provide that, and you'll definitely get the attention of the people at the big table with the checkbooks. The rule is:

Leaders want one-year payback from training.

The VP mentioned earlier had very specific numbers to achieve, so he created tactical training that moved the needle on his scorecard measures. He monetized those achievements and showed his leaders the results of their investment. What did he deliver?

In the first year alone, the additional new customers created a *70-times* one-year payback on his training investment. Plus, the ripple-through effect of these new sales generated tens of millions of dollars in margin over three years, all for a six-figure investment in training.

We admit, not every training project has one-year payback potential. But the more of those you can produce, the better off you will be at budget time. Here's how to make that happen.

◐ To Do

It's time to get out of the "Training is an important function within organizations" philosophical dead end and into the "Training made millions of dollars for the organization this year" game.

1. Get real. Training isn't a necessity. Remember the consulting firm from Chapter 2.2? It had no training function, yet it was experiencing steady growth. Accept the fact that nothing is guaranteed. You have to earn your keep every course, every year.

2. Change your mindset. You're not in the training business. You're in the scorecard needle-moving business. Training is nothing more than a Swiss Army Knife of profitability. Executives don't care if you're doing it with shamans and goat bones or wormholes

in inter-dimensional space. You are simply a set of tools that can be used to drive results. It's the old performance equation:

$$Knowhow + Focus + Motivation = Execution$$

Focus is the attention that will cause needles to move. Knowhow is provided by training and coaching. Motivation for learning is supplied by interesting content. The result is improved execution.

3. Start every discussion of training with questions that establish the benefit side of the payback equation:
   - What needle are we trying to move?
   - Where is it now?
   - Where does it need to be?
   - What must people do differently to get it there?
   - How soon does it need to happen?
   - What is the dollar benefit when it does?

   Yes, we understand that there will be training projects that are must-do's. But it is the wanna-do's that will keep your budget funds flowing. If you are helping the organization, your constituents will figure out some way to get you funding.

4. Continually analyze your results. Be diligent about computing payback numbers for every possible project. This is one of those "working ON the business" versus "working IN the business" training activities that often goes by the wayside when everyone gets busy. If you let that happen, you won't have any ammo come budget time.

5. Communicate your results to management. "Payback" is what you begin your annual update presentation with, not the typical litany of programs and student-days you provide.

Imagine starting your Update presentation with, "This year the Training department completely paid for itself by April 20th. Everything after that was profit to the organization, totaling $7 million." *That's* the kind of payoff required of Training.

The True Cost of Training

IN ORDER TO CALCULATE TRAINING'S NET VALUE to the organization, you need to have an accurate cost model. Ah, but the crafty training professional might make the observation that you don't want that cost model to be too comprehensive. After all, the more costs you overlook, the higher the value you show for training.

That sounds intriguing, until some busybody number cruncher points out that your total costs from the analyses are less than your actual departmental costs. That's when bad things start happening to crafty people.

There are important reasons why you don't want to hide training costs. First, you need to know your internal production costs so that you can properly scope and price projects. Without an accurate model, your cost estimates will be out of line or you'll exceed your budgets.

Second, without a model, you will have problems selecting the right deployment methods. What are the costs of classroom training versus e-learning? Of a conference call versus a webcast? Of click-and-read versus short-form video e-learning?

Third, a significant portion of the cost of training typically resides outside the Training department's budget. For example, travel expenses for classroom courses are training-related costs, but they may be buried in attendees' travel budgets.

Here is where that hurts you. Say you need development money to replace a classroom course with mobile e-learning. A comprehensive model can show why management should transfer some departmental travel budget money over to you, resulting in a net savings to the organization. Without that justification you're simply fighting for a budget increase, which is not going to happen. So you don't get the funds you need for the best solution, and the organization continues to spend more than it should on training without realizing it.

A comprehensive training model needs to include these costs:

Training-side costs. This includes Training department functions such as: needs analysis, design, development, instruction, administration, fulfillment, facilities, equipment, software, staff travel, content licensing, and contractors.

Organizational costs. This includes costs incurred by other departments in support of training such as: IT hosting and maintenance of a learning management system, IT help desk support for the Training department and learners, and learning center facilities and maintenance.

Learner-side costs. This includes costs such as: salary plus overhead for learning time plus travel time, travel costs, fees for outside training, and salary plus overtime for any replacement workers required during the training event.

These are all generally accepted direct costs of training and can usually be determined quite readily. But there is a potentially enormous cost that is rarely considered—the opportunity cost of learners.

We once facilitated a week-long training session for the entire enterprise sales force of a technology vendor, literally hundreds of people. Some of the attendees, disgruntled at being forced to sit in one place for a week, were trying to figure out how much the company was "wasting" on the training. It was a six-figure number which seemed reasonable.

This made us wonder about the impact of lost revenue from having no one out selling that week. So we passed around a sheet of paper and asked the attendees to simply write down their weekly quota. The total came to over $10 million.

This amount dwarfed the meeting costs yet was not even considered by the sales executives running the meeting. It never occurred to them to think of the opportunity cost of pulling their salespeople out of the market for a week. And this wasn't an isolated experience. We've seen companies schedule training right in the middle of their prime selling season and think nothing of it, never realizing what it was doing to their sales.

It's like scheduling training for CPAs during tax season. It isn't the cost of the training that matters. It isn't the payroll costs of the learner that hurts. It's the cost of the lost billings that really impacts the bottom line.

So we are back to our point at the start of this chapter. With full costs like these being recognized, why would leaders train anyone at all? From the organization's standpoint, it is easy to understand how executives can see Training as an expensive drain on resources. Yet as the agriculture case study from the previous chapter showed, even with a full cost model, training that is designed to move the scorecard needle on business results can still easily justify itself.

The problem is that the lack of an accurate training cost model delays the full-scale adoption of lower-cost, more effective, technology-based training solutions.

A recent survey found that 41% of learning executives still use classroom training as the primary learning delivery method for all content, and 65% use it for executive soft skills training.[1] They just don't realize how much the classroom training is costing them and what learning inefficiencies it creates.

◗ To Do

Build the financial analysis tools to help you make the right decisions:

1. Use your departmental data to develop true production cost models for the various modes of training you provide. These need to cover in-person and e-learning, both synchronous and asynchronous modes, and the various options for the physical delivery of content. Also make sure to include the complete range of costs such as those we mentioned earlier.

You don't have to create these models from scratch. A wide range of templates available on the Internet can give you a start. Our experience is that they aren't particularly comprehensive, but they can provide you with the major cost categories.

2. Create comparative training templates. You definitely need one for classroom versus e-learning, where classroom costs are fully identified. This will help your leaders see where the big dollars are going and help justify increasing your budget.

3. Share the data freely. Make this information a standard part of your executive updates. Everyone in the training process needs to understand the factors that affect costs and how you are managing them.

Determining the true cost of training is essential if you hope to accurately determine the true benefits of training.

2.6

How Do You Get People to Take Training?

ONE OF THE BIGGEST IRRITATIONS FOR TRAINERS is showing up for a class requiring a minimum of 10 attendees and finding five people sitting there. It's sometimes tough to fill classes, isn't it? And when you do fill them, people still don't come. In fact, a frustratingly high percentage of confirmed enrollees don't show up for class, don't dial into teleconferences, and don't log on to webcasts. Usually there is no notification that they aren't going to attend. And even when they do have the courtesy to cancel, it's often done at the last minute.

Remember that meeting with trainers and the outside expert? After discussing the question about how to get leaders to value training, the next discussion is invariably kicked off with Classic Question #2:

"How do I get people to take training?"

When trainers ask this, we figuratively put our arm around their shoulder, tell them we care about them and are concerned only for their welfare, request that they take this as helpful coaching feedback, then explain, "It's because your training is *terrible*."

We know that executives and managers need to get value from training. The third constituency for training departments is the obvious one, the learner. The answer to Classic Question #2 is:

It's all about compelling content.

As we talked about in Chapter 1.1, workplace learning is often plagued by the Terrible Too's. Training can be more of a punishment for employees than a development opportunity. There are too many topics where learners are asking themselves, "So what do I do now?" There is too much coma-inducing e-learning. There are too many webcasts where bored attendees are catching up on their e-mail during the session. There are too many death-by-*PowerPoint* classes where attendees in the back are reading *USA Today*. There is simply too big a gap between what learners need versus the content delivered. As a result, sometimes the whole system can be a dysfunctional joke.

Compelling content trumps all instructional design decisions. In fact, if the content is important enough, people learn even when there is *no* instructional design. They will grind through hundreds of poorly designed websites looking for information on health-related problems. They will spend hours researching a car purchase, laboriously scanning new and used car reviews and inventories. They will spend months learning about activities for an upcoming vacation, researching online, looking at guidebooks, and talking to friends.

Consider this. If someone asked you to pay $100 for a course on income taxes that guaranteed to save you $1,000 or else they'd pay you the $1,000, would you take that course? Of course you would. It wouldn't matter if the instructor was like the corny sports psychologist in *The Natural* ("Losing is a disease …")

This is not a hypothetical situation. One of the worst-presented, most boring video programs we have ever seen was a $100 course showing physicians how to save money on their taxes, and yet it still sold tens of thousands of copies. Why? Because the content was terrific.

So what is causing the problem in organizations?

First, organizations tend to teach employees things the *organization* wants them to know. Certainly, that's necessary, particularly when it comes to compliance topics. But organizations often don't teach things *employees* want to know, nor do they present valuable content in a manner that employees want to learn from.

Second, Training tends to create content by topic. So you get these generic program titles such as "Conflict Management," "Negotiating," or "Coaching." These are all important core skills, but they don't get at the specific needs of the targeted audience.

It's easy to get people to take training. Just communicate how it will *directly* help people deal with their problems, save them time and effort, make them money, or further their career.

Instead of "Conflict Management," they would rather learn "What to do when a customer is yelling at you." Instead of "Negotiating," they can make money with "How to win against the competition's two-for-one promotional offer." Instead of "Coaching," managers can enhance the performance of their department with "What to do when the job's not getting done." Yes, the core skills are buried in these courses, but the focus of the training is on a specific task that pays off for the learner.

You know you have compelling content when you don't have to coerce learners to attend training. Employees should be pounding on your desk *demanding* that they be given an attendance slot. They should be angry when others have received the training and they have not. If they aren't, then you know your content isn't right.

And don't try to claim that some content can't be made compelling. We've had managers explore sexual harassment training on their own because it was interesting and gave them new insights into communicating with their team members. It's all about the payoff to the learner.

◐ To Do

You need to take a candid look at your training and see if it is terrible from a learner standpoint:

1. Analyze attendance. Are you frequently cancelling classes? Do you have high no-shows for webcasts? Do you have to mandate training to get employees to actually show up? Can you only do training when people are already together at other events? Do you have to hound managers to send their subordinates? Do you have too many late cancellations and then have trouble getting those same people rebooked? These are all warning signs that you aren't delivering tangible value to the learner.

2. Sort your program topics into two categories. How many of them are things the organization wants workers to know? How many of

them are things you are certain that learners want to know? That "you are certain" phrase is key here. You can't be guessing about this. You must have solid data on learner needs and preferences. If nearly everything is driven by the organization, then that's a message for you.

3. Retitle your programs. Are you doing the typical training by topic, organizing content from a Training department standpoint? Or are you providing content from a learner application perspective? Use the benefit your learners receive from the content as the program title.

How do you get people to take training? It's all about compelling content that satisfies an unmet, urgent need.

See, Know, or Do Training

SO THE WAY TO GET EMPLOYEES TO TAKE TRAINING is to make certain the content is compelling. As we mentioned in the previous chapter, one problem is that Training departments deliver most of their content organized by topic. This complicates life for the learner and needs more discussion.

Consider the plight of a supervisor who has to give a low appraisal to a poor performer. She has a myriad of relevant classes at her disposal with titles such as DISC Tendencies, Conflict Management, Counseling Skills, The Coaching Process, Effective Writing, Employee Discipline Policies, Career Development, and Conducting Appraisals.

She has to not only complete all those individual courses but also consolidate the general principles taught between them, select the ones that fit her current situation, resolve any inconsistencies between them, and then figure out exactly how to apply them. Expecting a supervisor to do this, all while keep her department humming, is unrealistic. Why?

She may not have the time to complete all the relevant training. That's a lot of prep work to deal with a single appraisal, particularly if she has 10 other appraisals to do at the same time. And even if she did have the time, she has other ways to spend it that might actually drive business results.

It's asking a lot to expect a supervisor to integrate all that training and come up with a plan within the framework of a formal appraisal process. That's heavy-duty work even for someone who is a master of all those topics.

This is also extremely wasteful. She can't be the only supervisor who has ever had to review a poor performer. Why does each supervisor have to independently come up with an approach to what is a common problem? Why can't training that covers this specific situation be provided to anyone who requires it?

What all supervisors need is a "How to give a poor performer an appraisal" course. This program doesn't replace all of those other titles. In fact, it's a perfect supplement to them, helping supervisors apply the general concepts these courses teach. But this "How to ..." course has the benefit of not necessarily requiring them to have completed all those other programs. The "How to ..." program teaches just enough skills to let supervisors do this appraisal.

What we're saying is:

Training needs to be task-based.

Training programs have three kinds of goals. The first are "see" goals. You'll hear trainers say, "We're going to show them this," as if seeing content is learning it. This is the weakest of training goals.

If all you are going to do is show information to someone, then there are cheaper ways to do it than a learning event. Mail it to them. Ship a box of stuff to them. Assign it as reading. Put a poster up in the lunchroom. Do anything, but don't make people sit there like automatons while you flash information past their eyeballs. It's a total waste.

The second are "know" goals. You will hear trainers say, "They need to know this." This approach is often driven by subject matter experts who understand everything there is to know about a topic and are frustrated that everyone else knows so little. So you'll find programs covering details that none of the learners will actually use, like understanding the philosophy behind a pricing structure or having a product manufacturing process explained. It may even be interesting, but if no one is going to use the knowledge for anything, then it is still a weak goal.

The best are "do" goals. Here trainers ask, "What do we want the learners to *do differently* as a result of this training?" It also requires the follow-up question, "And how do those activities move the needle on our targeted business results?" Now you're talking about a strong training program goal.

A general sales skill course is important for reps to complete and provides core skills for winning complex orders. But a "How to win over the competition's two-for-one promotional offer" course tells salespeople exactly what you expect them to *do*.

It also gives you an opportunity to repeat core skill messages over and over again by applying them to different current high-priority situations. Through repetition, the skills are better internalized.

Those activities specifically move the needle on Competitive Win Rate and Market Share scorecard measures, which consequently drive Gross Revenue and Margin measures.

We agree that you need to train on general topics. But the real payoff comes from task-based training that directly targets the organizational initiatives that we have talked about, that helps managers deliver results, and that helps learners do their jobs better, faster, and easier. You need more task-oriented titles such as:

What to do when the job is not getting done
Handling the poor performer
Increasing productivity through praise
The daily management checklist
Protecting your PC from the bad guys
Writing effective e-mails
Reducing eye strain
How to host a business meal
Six wrong ways to manage
Managing people off site
First aid: cuts and scrapes
How to set sales call goals
Supervising a pronoid[1]

Then your executive, manager, and learner constituents can easily see exactly what value is being provided by the content.

○ **To Do**

Here is how to analyze the goals of your programs:

1. Go through your training topics again and take a "see, know, do" look at them. How many of them are simply showing content, and how many of them are teaching to a specific "do" goal? If you are like many organizations, you'll find that you are spending a lot of time on "see" and "know" training.

2. Take a similar look at your program titles. Are they longer programs covering many generic skills with little specific application training? Or are they targeted programs focused on "do" activities that move the needle on business results?

3. Look at the goals of each individual program. Check them for "see" and "know" wording versus "do" wording. If you find course goals terminology such as:

    Review …

    Understand …

    See how …

    Learn why …

    Identify the …

    Get an introduction to …

    Find out about …

    Increase awareness of …

    Become more sensitive to …

    Recognize the need for …

    See the importance of …

    Understand the rationale behind …

    Evaluate …

   and similar phrases, then the programs are focusing on "see" and "know" elements. Chances are your training is loaded with them.

   The general structure of a "do" goal is, "At the end of this program, you will be able to …" If programs are focused enough, the overall "do" goal may well be the course title itself. It's that simple.

What is the ultimate answer to the two classic questions
  trainers have?
How do I get management to *value* training?
How do I get people to *take* training?

It requires changing from programs with "see" and "know" goals to programs with "do" goals. It's making sure those "do" goals benefit learners and provide one-year payback for the organization. This will make the value of your training readily apparent to the folks at the big table who control your funding, and it will establish the Training department as a strategic resource in your organization.

Part 3

The Realities of Adult Learning

THE GOOD NEWS is that when it comes to any aspect of adult education, some researcher eager to get published has done a study on it. The result is an extensive body of knowledge on the factors involved in training workers and improving their performance.

The bad news is that either this research comes as a complete surprise to Training departments or that Training understands the issues but management totally ignores them.

In this part, we provide fundamental research on the realities of adult learning in organizations. For trainers new to these concepts, this will explain the issues. For trainers familiar with these concepts, this will provide proof sources to help you convince management that change is necessary.

The answers to these questions will have a profound effect on how your programs and services are designed and delivered moving forward:

How do adults learn, and what does that mean for Training?
What additions to existing training processes are required to drive actual performance improvement?

Avoiding Learner Overload

THE BOOK *EFFICIENCY IN LEARNING* contains quite an indictment of employee development:

> "Most organizational training courses incorporate much more content than human working memory can process in the time allotted."[1]

The results of this are catastrophic for learners.

Here is an analogy. Have you ever tried to pour a soda by dumping the contents of the bottle into a glass as fast as possible? You get a glass of foam and soda spilled all over. If you want a full glass, like it or not, you have to pour it slowly.

It's the same with pouring content into someone's brain. Functionally, people's minds work like the soda glass. If you overload learners, you don't get a partial result. You get nothing.

For example, give your telephone number to someone and he or she can repeat it back to you. But give this person your home, office, and cell numbers all at once, and he or she won't remember any of them. Their mental glass is empty due to overload.

Organizations need to recognize that learning requires mental effort and that people have a limited capacity for it. The amount of mental work learning generates is called "cognitive load."[2] This is a fundamental concept in employee training, yet organizations rarely pay attention to it.

Three types of cognitive load exist:

Content load. It takes more mental work to learn complex content. For example, calculus has a higher content load than arithmetic. Software troubleshooting has a higher content load than installing a USB printer. This is considered "unavoidable load" because it is based on the difficulty of the content itself.

Instruction load. This is the mental work created by the learning activities, which include understanding information, organizing it, and integrating it into memory. This is considered "good load."

Unnecessary load. This is irrelevant mental work created by the way content is taught. Boring *PowerPoint* presentations or screen-flipping CBTs generate unnecessary load. Funny stories that entertain but don't teach anything generate unnecessary load. This is considered "bad load."

Organizations mismanage cognitive load in a number of ways:
- Too long … 90-minute conference calls, 2-hour webcasts, 3-day sales meetings, 5-day seminars.
- Too much … 100+ slide *PowerPoint* presentations, 20 presentations over 2 days, 50-page reports.
- Too difficult … one-size-fits-all training where experts are bored and novices get overwhelmed.
- Too inefficient … fun content thrown in to maintain attention during overly long sessions, periodic activities inserted solely to get people moving and wake them up.

Unfortunately, management may not care about any of this. If they are going to spend big money to bring people together for some learning event—whatever the medium—then they are going to throw as much information as possible at attendees in the time available so that the event is more "cost-effective." What they don't realize is that by overloading learners, they end up accomplishing nothing.

If you want the Training department to be successful, then you must become the advocate for controlling the cognitive load of learning. You need to be that proverbial voice in the wilderness asking tough questions such as:

"How much is enough? How many presentations can they endure before they hit overload?"

"How fast is too fast? Do we really think 'drinking from the fire hose' actually works?"

"How long do we have before they are 'stick a fork in them' worn out and done?"

What can we realistically teach them in the time we have?"

Admittedly, this does not make you particularly popular with management. They are only thinking about shoving the maximum amount of content at workers for the minimum cost. Actual learning isn't part of the equation.

Management is only thinking in terms of "see" goals, which will have little effect on organizational results. If this is all that's required, then there are much better ways to accomplish "see" goals than training events.

But if results are needed, you must keep everyone focused on "do" goals that move the needle on scorecard measures. That requires making sure the cognitive load for learners is within their capabilities.

◯ To Do

This is a fundamental concept you need to make sure everyone understands.

1. Educate your Training team on the principles of cognitive load. Make certain your teams and management know how adult learning works, as well as how cognitive load capacities differ between experts and novices.

2. Get your own house in order first. Look at your existing programs and analyze them on the basis of the research here in Part 3. If your offerings are similar to the list mentioned earlier, you may

discover that *none* of your programs are realistic in terms of cognitive load and that they *all* suffer from the Terrible Too's.

3. Be the voice of reason when events are being planned, especially when the responsibility for success will be put on Training. Keep management focused on what they want participants to *do* as a result of the experience, not on how much the organization can dump on them at one time.

   If management listens to you, great. You have done your organization and its learners a real service. If management doesn't listen, you have at least provided the best professional advice you can. And you have also gone on record ahead of time in case the results are disappointing.

4. Use the instructional design principles in this book to lighten content load, eliminate unnecessary load, and optimize the instructional load of your programs.

An adage about training states, "The mind can absorb only what the bottom can endure." Now you know better. The mind can absorb only what the mind can absorb. Your job is to make certain the cognitive load of training stays within that limit.

How Working Memory Works

AS TRAINERS, A LOT OF WHAT WE DO to increase learning actually has the opposite effect.

One of the most common methods of teaching is to read text content to learners. In a live session, this is the classic back-to-audience style in which a presenter reads slides to the attendees. In e-learning, this is the traditional click-and-read approach in which a disembodied narrator reads the onscreen text word for word. Learners universally agree that this is a mind-numbing way to be taught, researchers recommend against it, yet the practice is still popular with instructional designers and trainers.

The rationale behind reading text content to learners is the assumption that you accommodate both visual and verbal learning styles. In reality, this is another one of those training myths like those we talked about in Chapter 1.2.

The narration of onscreen text can actually reduce learning by overloading the limited capacity of something called "working memory."[1]

Learning requires taking information from short-term or working memory and integrating it into longer-term memory. Working memory holds about four to seven items and lasts for about 10 seconds.[2] The Baddeley model states that working memory actually consists of four separate components, with two of those components of particular interest to trainers.[3]

Audio loop. This deals with the sounds or language we hear. Think of it as a very short recorder where audio information is momentarily placed. The information is quickly lost as it is overwritten by new sounds. You can retain what is in your audio loop by putting it into longer-term memory, or you can temporarily keep it alive through repetition, like saying a phone number you just looked up over and over until you make the call.

Visual sketchpad. This deals with what we see, which includes visual, spatial, and movement components. This is what we use to remember images, shapes, colors, location and speed of objects, and movements such as driving or making your way through a sea of office cubicles.

The startling finding for trainers is that these two components of working memory operate independently of each other.

For example, researchers found that when people were asked to do a primary audio task (recall a list of numbers read out loud) and a secondary audio task (respond to a tone), performance on one or both tasks suffered. But when the second task was visual (tracing a moving dot), there were minimal declines in performance.[4]

In general, when learning tasks utilize the same mode, performance plummets. Our capacity for learning with multiple messages to the same component of working memory is very limited.

So let's get back to the original situation—the verbatim reading of onscreen text. It has a number of characteristics that depress learning:

1. The narration is not providing information different from the text. Both are simply duplicating their content in a second medium. So the simultaneous processing capability of working memory is not being utilized.
2. The two inputs come in at different speeds. We speak at about 150 words per minute, and the average adult reads at 250 words per minute with a 70% comprehension rate.[5] Learners waste mental resources trying to synchronize the slow narration to their faster reading rate.
3. Learners can become distracted by focusing on doing a word-for-word comparison of the text and narration. They find themselves looking for discrepancies between the two versions versus paying attention to the content itself.

4. When graphics or animations are also involved, there are then three inputs to working memory. Narration takes up the audio loop, and the graphic and text conflict with each other for the visual sketchpad. This is why research shows that you are better off explaining visual content with audio narration than with text.[6]

The message is that you have to be aware of the memory limitations of learners. Training must properly utilize the independent components of working memory while making sure each of them are not individually overloaded.

▷ To Do

Along with cognitive load, working memory is another fundamental concept your entire Training department must understand.

1. Educate your Training team on the principles of working memory. Make sure everyone understands the audio loop and the visual sketchpad, as well as how they function independently.
2. Examine your design guidelines and practices. Are these adult learning principles reflected in them? Do designers understand the ramifications of violating these practices?
3. Review your current training offerings. Do you utilize the classic click-and-read model where static slides contain text and graphics and there is narration and sound effects? Are you overloading learners' visual sketchpad and/or audio loop with multiple inputs?
4. Take a current project and implement it according to these principles. Use that as a pilot to verify the effects on learners from a results and satisfaction standpoint.

A preschooler once said, "Memory is what I forget with." You now know how to make memory theory a powerful tool in creating effective learning offerings.

Pay Attention to Attention

THE SCIENCE OF ATTENTION is the next critical factor in adult learning that is typically ignored by organizations.

Years ago when we were doing live TV satellite training, everything had to be an hour long. That was how much satellite time the client had bought and, by gum, they were going to get their money's worth. The sessions felt long for us to teach, seemed tedious to sit through for students, and overall they weren't very popular.

When we shifted over to Internet delivery of video-based training, we thought we'd be geniuses and cut the sessions down to 30 minutes. We still received feedback that they were too long. So we cut back to 20 minutes, which was still getting complaints. When we finally got down to around 10 minutes, it was just right. As we dug into research on learning and attention span, we found out why.

You may already be doing everything else right. You are creating engaging training that has value for the organization. It is task oriented. You are not generating excessive cognitive load. You are utilizing the simultaneous power of working memory subsystems and are not individually overloading them. Yet you are still not getting results. What's going on? It may be a matter of attention.

What is the average length of a classroom training program at your organization? Half day? Full day? Multiple days? How long are your e-learning courses? 60 minutes? 90 minutes? How long do webcasts or conference calls last? One hour? Two hours?

You have to ask yourself if it is reasonable to expect that people will actually pay attention continually throughout these events. The answer is, "No."

Forget the issue of cognitive load for now. The fact is that lengthy learning events like these totally ignore the research on adult attention span. There are three important factors that trainers have to acknowledge.

(1) Learners have a short attention span.

Here is a cross-section of the research:

- Behavioral psychologists suggest that people are programmed to maintain attention for 7 minutes. Why? That's the average time between commercials.[1]
- Informal surveys of e-learning designers indicate that online students have between 5 and 15 minutes' worth of attention for self-study lessons.[2]
- After 3 to 5 minutes of settling down at the start of a class, the next lapse of attention occurs between 10 and 18 minutes later. As the lecture proceeds, attention span shortens to 3 or 4 minutes by the end of a standard lecture, with the rate of decrease higher for complex content.[3]
- Students recall the most information from the first 5 minutes of a presentation. Impact declines over the next 10 minutes, with the lowest point the 15-to 20-minute mark.[4]
- A survey of 1,000 university students in England found the average length of time they could concentrate in lectures was 10 minutes.[5]

So a good assumption is that basic learner attention span is somewhere between 5 and 15 minutes in duration.

(2) The work environment breaks up attention.

The typical workplace environment forces short attention spans. This is due to the frequency of interruptions and the number of simultaneous tasks being done at any point in time.

The study referenced at the end of Chapter 1.2 found that workers spent on average 11½ minutes in continuous work on a project or theme before they switched to something else. Single project work was fragmented into even shorter 3-minute tasks.[6] Clearly, it's difficult to pay attention to anything for an extended period of time in today's work environment. There's just too much else going on.

(3) Full attention is rare.
It happens all the time. You see drivers texting on their phones. While people are talking to you, they are looking over your shoulder listening in on a nearby conversation. Your significant other listens to you while watching TV. You handle your e-mail while you're on a webcast. At any one moment, you are paying attention to a variety of inputs, and there are plenty of them in today's world.

Microsoft researcher Linda Stone has observed:

"We live in a continuous state of partial attention."[7]

This is different than multi-tasking, where full attention purposefully shifts between a set of activities. Partial attention is when you skim the surface of incoming content, pick out the relevant information, and then quickly move on to another input stream. It seems like people today never pay full attention to anything.

You experience it in classrooms when attendees in the back row are reading their *USA Today* or when students are checking phone messages, handling e-mails, or filling out their expense reports. It's a rare presentation moment when the entire group is fully engaged.

(4) The trend is ever shorter content.
So far we have been talking about the research on attention. A final factor to keep in mind is learner preferences. The trend is for content to be shorter and shorter.

Some people are now suggesting that the maximum length of content should be no longer than the average music video—no more than three or four minutes. Video highlights of big events such as the Olympics were typically 60 to 90 seconds long.

Keep in mind, as long as the content is complete and effective, people are not going to complain that they wanted it to spend more time on it.

Let's go back to the lengths of all that learning you are offering. One hour? Two hours? Multiple days? Are you kidding? The reality is that it's a fantasy to think you are going to maintain your learners' full attention for that long. They can give you a maximum of around 5 to 15 minutes at a time, and that's about it.

Some trainers have finally accepted this as a fact of life that cannot be ignored. As a result, they have completely re-architected their learning content into discrete chunks approximately 10 minutes or less in length. They can easily handle single learning points with programs this short. Complex subjects can be organized into a series of programs, each standing on its own but still part of an overall sequence.

One obvious ramification is that this essentially mandates the use of e-learning because that is the only way to efficiently deploy content this short. But that actually creates additional benefits, which we'll talk about in Part 5.

The result of adopting this 10-minute maximum target is usually a surge in satisfaction with training:

Learners love it because they can easily fit training into their work day. Content comes at them in digestible chunks with very targeted "do" goals for follow-up.

Managers love it because short content like this can be inserted into team or departmental meetings and then used later with individual coaching. Ten minutes of learning and 10 minutes of debrief, and it's back to the regular meeting agenda.

Instructional designers love it because it's a joy to focus on a specific learning point, teach it well, and then move on.

An old saying in sports is, "You have to take what the defense gives you." In this case, you have to design your training to the realistic attention you can hope to get from learners. Trying to jam 50 minutes of content into a 5- to 15-minute attention span doesn't help anybody. It just makes your learning more inefficient.

◌ **To Do**

There's not a lot to decide, but there's a lot to be done concerning the realities of attention.

1. Review all the research you can find on adult learning attention span. Make sure you have proof sources ready for skeptics.
2. Review your program standards. Are your offerings too long to be effective?
3. Make a decision on whether you are going to accept the 10 minutes or less target as an inescapable fact of life in training or whether you will continue to ignore it and keep dumping content on fatigued or distracted learners.
4. Either way, start designing your training with the reality of attention in mind.

You have to pay attention to attention. You're not accomplishing anything if nobody is listening.

Don't Forget Forgetting

WHEN YOU ASK MANAGERS about the competence of their people, you often hear them say something like, "Oh, we trained employees on that two years ago."

We don't know about you, but we have trouble remembering what we had for lunch two weeks ago, much less stuff from some course we sat through two years ago. We're lucky if we can even recall going to a program. "Have I attended Advanced Advancing II? Uh, I think so. I'll have to go through my binder collection to know for sure."

Thank goodness the medical community doesn't use this approach. It would be just our luck to have a heart attack and get rescuers who had CPR training 10 years ago or who had been hired after the CPR training event was held. When they blow on our chest and push on our face because they've forgotten what to do, we're goners.

Most organizations are totally focused on initial training (i.e., "acquisition learning"). They operate on the false assumption that once you train employees on a topic, they have mastered it forever. Nothing could be further from the truth. The unavoidable reality is:

Single event training doesn't work.

It never has worked and it never will work because it totally ignores the follow-up side of the training process (i.e., "refresh learning").

In general, we remember little or nothing of what we experience daily unless we do something with that information. (The only exception is for highly emotional events. Life creates those, not trainers.) Forgetting is a fact of life that trainers need to quit ignoring.

When it comes to forgetting, several factors are at work. Research indicates that it is primarily a matter of interference. Life's steady stream of new information overlays whatever came just before it.

A second factor is the lack of retrieval cues. This is the "on-the-tip-of-my-tongue" situation where you know that you know something, but you can't retrieve it from memory.

Don't get caught up in trying to find specific percentages for how much people forget and over what periods of time. Too many factors are involved, and the research numbers are all over the place depending upon the situation. In general, what we do know is:

- People forget lots of information soon after learning it, but over time the pace of forgetting slows (the so-called Forgetting Curve).[1]
- Facts and procedural skills are more susceptible to forgetting.[2]
- Learning time is reduced, and retention is increased by reviews spaced out over time (the Spacing Effect.)[3]

These last two are key learning points for training professionals, and lead to an important question:

"What is your refresh learning strategy?"

This is guaranteed to generate a blank look from trainers whose departments provide a giant collection of one-and-done offerings. This is a question they have never been asked, about an issue they have never even considered.

Contrast this with the medical community, in which mastery of a skill is critical. In our earlier example, every medical professional is required to periodically take CPR review courses. Medical trainers understand retention. It's a life or death issue.

You can't expect learners to remember the Six Buying Influences or the Five-Step Conflict Management Process after seeing them once and never again hearing them mentioned. And it doesn't matter how much in-program practice there is. A single event does not lead to long-term mastery. There needs to be a refresh learning process to remind employees of what they learned and reinforce its usage on the job.

In fact, given a limited budget, we can make a strong argument from a research standpoint that it would be more effective to eliminate all single-event acquisition training and focus solely on providing the associated refresh learning. You would get better results because employees would actually remember something over time.

Look through your current program offerings. How many are focused on refreshing critical skills that have already been taught? This is not going through the original event again. That's too inefficient. Ideally, it should be a short-form version of the original content.

Do you have titles such as "Review of No-Push Selling" or "Process Improvement Team Skills for Experienced Team Members," and so on? If not, it's an indicator that you don't have a refresh learning strategy in place.

When separate programs are not possible, look at your method of delivery. Does your online training allow re-learners to quickly review the original content, like moving a video slider and pausing where needed? Or are re-learners stuck having to click through a 100-slide sequence with a mandatory time delay between slides?

You can't ignore this issue and expect to succeed as a Training department. Remember, single-event training doesn't work. Acquisition learning and refresh learning are two different processes, and you need them both.

○ To Do

You need to include refresh learning into your overall training strategy:

1. Build a master list of every training event, course, and product your department offers.
2. Prioritize this list to identify high-value skills.
3. Indicate for each priority offering whether it is acquisition learning, refresh learning, or both. It is both when there is an established process in place for learners to review the original training again.

4. For your high-priority skills, create specific refresh learning offerings.
5. For all offerings, use a course deployment technology that allows experienced learners to quickly review content.

You can't forget about forgetting. You don't want your employees figuratively pushing on each other's faces and blowing on their chests. (Note to self: Reread this chapter in six months.)

The Problem of Anticipation Learning

Q: WHAT TRAINING IS THE BIGGEST WASTE of time for learners?
A: A one-day *Excel* class.

We've all been forced to take it some time or another. Heck, some of us have had to teach it, too. It's that software training class taught in a computer lab full of PCs. You spend the day explaining arcane commands and wandering around helping students with happy fingers dig their way out of menu hierarchy messes. By the end of the course, your attendees are supposedly ready to do spreadsheet battle. They are setting up complex formulas, automating tasks with macros, using pivot tables. They are pushing *Excel* to its limits with confidence.

Then everybody goes back to their jobs. Voice mail is maxed out. Their e-mail inbox is several screens long. Work is backed up. The boss is asking when key reports will be finished. Life is back to normal and then some because the attendees have been away for a day.

About a month or so after the training, a co-worker comes up to one of your graduates asking how to set up a pivot table and a pivot chart report. In the time since class, the Forgetting Curve has been steadily at work. All those commands, if they haven't already been totally forgotten, are now a confused jumble of menu options. Your student has to go back to the *Excel* help system to even remember what tab the pivot table menu sequence resides in.

Sound familiar? This happens with more than just PC skills training. It occurs with any content that involves detailed information and complex processes or has intervals so long between performance repetitions that the methods are forgotten in between.

But we just talked about this in the previous chapter on forgetting. The answer to this is supposed to be a refresh learning process, right? It turns out that there is certain content where that isn't enough. Unless delivery methods are changed, even refresh learning is still delivered periodically, which may not be sufficient for some tasks.

The problem is that most training is "anticipation learning" (i.e., content delivered long before employees actually need it). Like in the *Excel* example, this gives the Forgetting Curve time to do its work, where the bulk of that forgetting happens soon after the training event. If those new skills are not immediately used on the job, or if a refresh learning event doesn't take place in the interim, new skills are lost and have to be re-taught.

Contrast this with training that focuses on learning at the point of need, so-called teachable moments.[1] What's required is content with four "right" characteristics:

Right need.
Training is most effective when it is delivered to address a worker need. Learning how to do a pivot table might be useful, but if none of the Advanced *Excel* Training attendees actually need to create a pivot table when they return to their jobs, then it's not compelling content.

Right time.
Training is most effective when it is delivered *immediately* when needed. By that, we mean within seconds. That's the only way to defeat the Forgetting Curve. Even a one-day class has an overnight usage delay built in, with the inevitable loss of a significant portion of the information. Remember, the largest block of forgetting happens right after the training event.

Right amount.
Trainers tend to clump huge amounts of content into learning events in order to completely cover a topic and all its ramifications. It's

supposedly the "efficient" way to teach. But most learners find only a small part of it helpful.

That's why you so often hear attendees say something like, "It was a useful seminar. I got two or three really good ideas out of it."

Sixteen hours spent to get a couple of useful ideas? Are you kidding? You could have conveyed that in 10 minutes. How can the Training function survive with such inefficiencies?

Workers want to learn just enough for the task at hand, do it, and then go on to the next job. They don't want a history of electricity starting with an ancient Egyptian battery. They just need to safely install a replacement compressor pump. All that other information might be useful someday, but they know they won't remember it by the time they're in the same situation again.

Right design.

Employees simply need help. They want training that is easy to learn from, that can be taken right at the point of application, and that can be completed quickly. This is training with the very attributes we have been talking about—compelling, task-oriented, results focused, and short. And if it is to be delivered at every possible point of use, it has to be designed for deployment to mobile devices.

Reducing program length is not just about cognitive load and attention span. The issue of anticipation learning is one more reason why training needs to be designed to no more than a 5 to 15 minute target time. It's the perfect format for "right" learning.

Let's go back to our Advanced *Excel* training example. Instead of sending people to training in a PC lab, what should organizations do? Online *Excel* training courses are hours in length, more complicated than a classroom course because there is no wandering tutor to help, and just as forgettable as the computer lab version. *Excel's* online help system may not provide enough information for users to figure it out on their own, and an Internet search often turns up an overwhelming amount of sometimes conflicting information.

The best solutions are CBT products that have divided up all the functions of software such as *Excel* into hundreds of short training programs. Each teaches a single task and shows the operations in a screen capture window. Learners can place the course window and their own application window side by side and follow the tutorial, stopping it when needed to actually perform the functions as they are being shown.

What we're talking about here is a blurring of training and performance support. Ideally, both of these functions can be done with the exact same training products. This is an important "multi-purposed learning" topic that we will address in Part 6.

With solutions like these, it's not a matter of remembering at all. Once a task is completed, employees can forget about how to do it, knowing that they can quickly re-teach themselves should they need to do it again.

▷ To Do

We know we keep sending you back to review your existing training offerings and upcoming projects. That is going to continue throughout the book.

1. Go back through your master list of training offerings and identify the difficult content that has a high content cognitive load for learners. It could be soft skills programs such as a Key Account Selling process, or it could be hard skills training such as The Truck Safety Check Process.

2. Refresh learning may not be enough for some of your high content load topics like these. Determine where performance gaps exist and what the high-payback tasks are.

3. Identify when and where employees need to know how to complete these priority processes. Compare that with the anticipation training you are currently offering. Is there a fundamental disconnect there, such as with the Advanced *Excel* Training course?

4. Choose a high-payback opportunity and pilot the "right" approach.
5. On the basis of what you learn from the pilot, integrate this philosophy into your overall training strategy.

We have a saying, "Without a need, don't proceed." Anticipation training focuses on projected needs and may not make a lasting difference regardless of your refresh learning process. "Right" learning delivers on immediate performance needs.

Part 4

Instructional Design That Works

YOU HAVE SEEN THE RESEARCH in Part 3 on adult learning. The same situation exists for instructional design. All the rules for constructing effective learning have been similarly researched and address these key questions:

How do you apply the research on adult learning
  to organizational training?
How can your training be more effective?
What may you be doing wrong?
What are ways to lower training costs and still
  improve results?

The Three-Level Model for Customizing Training

ENDLESS AMOUNTS OF TRAINING PRODUCTS are available today, and they come in a variety of classroom and distance learning formats. A question instructional designers face is how to customize off-the-shelf training for their organization's specific needs. The method most often used is actually driven by vendor sales strategies and may not fit what research indicates is the best way to teach content.

Suppose your organization really likes OhWow Leadership from DanKenCo Training, but it needs to be tailored. DanKenCo proposes modifying its general terminology where needed and replacing all the examples and exercises throughout the entire program—all for a convenient six-figure fee. This is a common vendor practice, and one that purchasers of third-party training products are comfortable with. The result is a totally custom course based on the core principles of OhWow Leadership.

The problem is that this fails to take into account some important factors in the way people learn—factors that can also be used to significantly reduce costs.

Training is typically offered as one-size-fits-all. Every student is assumed to be a novice on the topic at hand, and only a single version of a course is provided. This means that 20-year expert employees end up mixed in with new hires in a training program paced somewhere in the middle. As a result, new hires are overwhelmed and experienced employees are bored. Something has to change.

Novices versus experts.

Research suggests that one size actually does not fit all and that novices need to be trained differently than experts. Novices require a more controlled cognitive load because everything is new to them. Their training needs to be shorter and more directive, with steps, examples, and structured practice. This is fundamental "know" content that is supported by diagrams and text. Also, visuals are more helpful for novices.[1]

Some research indicates that techniques that are effective for novices can actually *reduce* learning in experts.[2] High-knowledge learners have a wider range of prior experience, which allows them to learn faster. You should drop either the diagram or the text in visuals, depending on which one is necessary to complete the task. You can transition faster from worked examples to full practice exercises. And interactions may not add much to the learning process for experts.

Segmented content.

You need to segment content differently than you do now. You know that it is important to control the cognitive load for novices. One method that increases learning in novices is to teach the basic concepts separately before teaching the main content.[3] This provides the fundamental background knowledge that experts already have and helps reduce the amount of complex information novices receive at one time.

This means you should teach the names and functions of the components in a process *before* you teach the process steps themselves. You should teach support knowledge such as the reasons for a task or knowledge supporting the task *separately* before teaching the skill required for the task.[4]

The customization process described earlier essentially ignores this research by lumping all the training on OhWow Leadership into one program and then providing full practice examples after each block of the content has been initially taught.

There needs to be a way to meet the need for custom content while accommodating the requirements of novice learners, as well as a way to not waste the time of experienced learners. It also needs to be done without having to create two versions of every training program, which is cost prohibitive and impractical. In addition, it would be great to avoid spending large sums to customize existing training programs, either internal or external.

The three-level content model.

One method to do this is to adopt a three-level content structure. In this model, Level 1 addresses basic concepts that apply to any organization. This is off-the-shelf content that is never customized. Examples are an "Introduction to Negotiating" sequence or a "DISC Personality Tendencies" series.

Level 2 is custom content that assumes learners have completed the associated Level 1 programs. It applies Level 1 concepts to specific tasks in an individual organization. So it is a mix of the vendor's (or Training department's) intellectual property from the Level 1 training and the proprietary information of the organization. An example might be a "How to Counter a Competitor's Two-for-One Promo Offer" that uses the terminology and techniques of generic Level 1 negotiating training.

Level 3 is totally custom content that applies specifically to an organization. It is one-of-a-kind training and contains no Level 1 content. This three-level approach allows you to better meet learner requirements. Novices can begin with the Level 1 content and work up through Level 2. Experts can go directly to Level 2 content and do a quick refresh if needed on supporting Level 1 content.

There are also significant cost savings in using a three-level approach:

- There is no need to create separate versions of programs for novices and experts.
- Experts don't waste time in basic concepts training programs. They also spend less time overall in learning and learn better while they are there.
- Third-party content obtained from vendors, as in the off-the-shelf OhWow Leadership example, doesn't have to be customized from front to back at high additional fees.

- The development effort to create a few supplemental Level 2 programs is typically far less than having to completely customize an entire Level 1 training program.

One thing to be aware of is who owns what content. Level 1 content is typically owned by the originator. In the case of third-party training vendors, this is content that they own and license to clients. It goes away when the vendor goes away.

Because there is proprietary content from both parties in Level 2, this content likely also goes away when the vendor goes away. The vendor can no longer use the program, but neither can the organization. This is true even if the client paid for the development, unless there are contract provisions to the contrary.

Level 3 content is typically developed by the vendor as work-for-hire, and is totally owned by the organization since there is no vendor content included.

Another thing to note is that this same structure can be used within the Level 1 training sequence itself, which is a good overall instructional design philosophy. For example, in teaching a Conflict Management series, an initial program might cover the psychology of conflict before teaching the conflict management steps themselves. This helps control cognitive load for all students regardless of their experience level.

◌ To Do

Use this three-level model to efficiently segment your training and get the most out of your third-party training content.

1. Candidly examine your training offerings and identify your approach to the novice/expert training issue. Are you designing all training for novices? Are you trying to go novice-to-expert in one training session and generating too much cognitive load? Are you aiming at the middle and missing both audiences?
2. Review how you are working with vendors. Are you paying to transform complete courses? Or are you using their generic content and then developing a smaller amount of custom Level 2 content that leverages their concepts?

3. Analyze the opportunities you have to both lower costs and increase training effectiveness through a three-level content approach, and then try it with a new training assignment.

A three-level content structure can help Training departments deal with the wide variety of existing student skill levels. It allows trainers to better leverage off-the-shelf content, improve learning, and save money while doing it.

Choosing a Backbone

WE HAVE ALL HAD THE EXPERIENCE of completing a training program and asking ourselves, "What did I just learn?" Plenty of information was provided, and it seemed useful somehow, but then we struggled with how it all fit together and where to pack it away in long-term memory. When this happens, it's often a problem with how the content is organized.

One of the biggest challenges trainers face is coming up with the specific structure for a new program. There is a generally accepted flow for training that includes modules such as introduction, goals, content, practice, evaluation, and wrap-up. But that "content" module is the big one.

Course authors typically start with an overabundance of resources when it comes to source material. There might be an existing but out-of-date course. There is a host of job and process documentation. There is performance management information. There may be competency lists. There might be a needs analysis or workplace survey results. There is everything imaginable about the topic on the Internet, including sample courses from a variety of sources. The challenge is to organize all this into a coherent flow for learners.

As a result, an important first question for course designers to consider is, "What is the backbone?" By backbone, we mean the under-lying structure for the entire course. This is the fundamental structure that will be used to help learners understand and remember the content. Training is essentially helping learners integrate new information into their existing store of knowledge. That is one of the reasons why experts learn faster. They have more existing knowledge that they can connect new information to.

Types of Backbones.
When it comes to organizing content, common structures create familiar ways to retain information in long-term memory. Here are some popular backbones:

Process. This is one of the most frequently used content structures in training. Any task can be broken down into a series of steps. Learners can then create a mental model of actually completing the task, whether it is something physical such as repairing a forklift or something logical such as posting an order to an online system.

Chronology. Another common backbone is the time sequence … this happens on date one, this happens on date two, and so on. In essence, the clock or a calendar provides the structure.

Topology. Content can be organized by spatial relationships. The flow is … here, then here, then here. This could be a lecture on anatomy using a picture of the body. It could be the layout of a warehouse in talking about product flow. Or it could be a virtual stroll through an office space.

Pairs. Sometimes content is not particularly sequenced and is more list-like in nature. In this case you might be able to use a paired-sequence backbone, which includes question-answer, problem-solution, objection-response, feature-advantage, feature-by-feature product comparisons, and so on.

Regardless of the pair structure chosen, these lists should be sequenced in some sort of logical manner if at all possible. This could be by importance, priority, frequency, effect on satisfaction, interest, applicability (i.e., any logical rationale learners can identify with). That makes the content easier to remember than random pairs of items.

Change of position. This is similar to a pair structure, except that this backbone is focused on a mindset. The theme is, "You are over there now, and you should be over here." This backbone could be used for attitudes, beliefs, decisions, strategies (i.e., any situation where you need to make a structured argument as to why someone should change their thinking about a topic).

Mystery trip. This is actually an anti-structure that makes use of the universal appeal of curiosity. A business book editor once told us that it can be useful to lead people on a "magical tour of your ideas," much like a novelist. A mystery trip can take people down a thought chain with an unknown end, with the sheer novelty keeping their attention. The good news is that this can be very powerful. The bad news is that you can't do it for long without frustrating the learner, so its primary use is for shorter content.

As a note, it is possible to utilize more than one backbone. For example, you might combine a feature comparison (pairs) with a physical review of the products (topology). Or you might combine a process backbone with chronology, where a series of tasks are time dependent. The important point is that a familiar structure should be present and obvious.

Common Backbone Mistakes

A number of mistakes can be made with training program backbones.

The first is faulty logic. For example, a sales call is always taught as a linear process. The typical flow is something such as open, question, sell, handle objections, and close. Yet research suggests that sales calls rarely follow that pattern. Good salespeople do all those things, but they do them in a different order call-to-call, depending upon what prospects want to talk about.[1] So the chronology backbone typically used for sales process training actually forces course authors to exclude this important factor in selling.

The second mistake is a faulty analogy. Sometimes the backbone is just too big a stretch for the content. For example, "How is surgery like a car?" OK, this is comparing an unfamiliar surgery to something familiar like a car, but the analogy is flawed. One is an event, and the other is a piece of equipment. Students spend more time trying to figure out the connections between the two than learning the content itself.

The third mistake is a weak backbone. For example, we have had several clients use their company name as the memory acronym for sales process steps. Unfortunately, the letters didn't fit the process words they were forced to use.

In one case, the Prepare step became "blueprint" because they needed a "B." Then, to make the acronym work, the classic Sell step was changed into two steps, "support" and "collaborate." So the overall sales process being taught became *more* difficult to learn because of the acronym, not easier.

With all three of these mistakes, the backbone increases the cognitive load on the learner, which is exactly the opposite of what it's supposed to do.

▷ To Do

Pre-organizing content in a way already familiar to learners will help drive content retention rates up.

1. Begin the design process by asking, "What do the learners already know that we can leverage?" New products can use existing products as the familiar reference point. Business situations can be compared to similar problems in personal life, and so on.
2. Have the backbone discussion early in the training design process. It provides the foundation for everything that follows.
3. Validate the backbone with potential learners. Check the backbone's logic, analogy, and ease of use to make certain it supports learning rather than makes it more difficult. The problem with the force-fit acronym words would have been immediately identified this way.
4. Be willing to change the backbone right away if it isn't working out.

The greatest tool instructional designers have is what employees already know. Building training with a clear structure helps learners remember faster and retain more.

4.3

The No B.S. Rule

HAVE YOU EVER BEEN ASKED to create training for an initiative that looks suspiciously like a previous program that was a total failure? What the *Dilbert* cartoon crew described as something like a dead woodchuck?[1] Maybe it was even a series of woodchucks such as quality circles that grew into total quality management that jumped to reengineering that morphed into outsourcing that became rightsizing.

Now your assignment is to take this next project and, with a straight face, train employees on how it's a wonderful new thing that will totally transform the organization. You know what the reaction is going to be. Outside, employees will be calmly sitting through the training, but inside, you know they'll be thinking, "What a joke."

This is a serious issue for you as a trainer. It is unavoidable, and it will sink your training effort if you fail to address it. Unfortunately, many organizations don't want to hear this, and they certainly don't want to talk about it. Management has a warped Home On the Range attitude: "Never is heard a discouraging word, and the sky had better not be cloudy all day." The last thing leaders want you to do is acknowledge past failures, lest anyone be made to look bad.

From a strategic standpoint, this isn't going to work because it is a violation of important core values. The Baldrige Award folks address this with their "valuing workforce members and partners" and "management by fact" values.[2] Their theme is that excellence requires maintaining an engaged workforce and being straightforward about the measurement of performance.

For us, it is our company value of "candid communication." Our standard is to be open, frank, and honest and not waste time dancing around the real issues.

The "no discouraging words" attitude is also not going to work from a training standpoint, because it immediately turns employees off. They're thinking, "You expect us to believe this propaganda?" Or they figure, "Management is clueless." Either way, their reaction is that leaders don't get it, which is one of the symptoms of a dysfunctional organization that we talk about in Chapter 7.4. And if you're following the party line, by extension, they think that you don't get it either.

This then becomes an elephant in the room that nobody wants to talk about, but everyone knows is there. And until you deal with this elephant, your training is going nowhere.

When you are faced with situations like these, it's crucial to teach with the "voice of the learner." What we mean by that is you have to acknowledge what learners are thinking going into the training—whether you like it or not. You need to take any bad history and the accompanying skepticism head-on and do it right up front. It's the *No B.S. Rule*, where you are addressing exactly what your learners are thinking.

If a new initiative looks like a stale update on a string of abandoned fads, then you might include this in your opening: "I don't know about you, but when I first saw this Commitment to Quality initiative, it seemed to me that it looks just like the Excellence in Everything program we tried a few years back. Is that what you're thinking? Because that's how it looked to me at first."

This creates something we call nod momentum, where learners are thinking, "Uh, yeah … that's exactly the way it looks." Employees realize that you get it, and that you aren't going to dodge what is obvious to everyone. They appreciate that you are willing to take on the big issue. The result is that they are curious about what you have to say next.

Now you can continue, "But when I really looked at it, I saw a lot of differences in the Commitment to Quality process. We've taken past lessons to heart this time around. Let me show you how it works, from leadership involvement on down, and then see what you think…"

The No B.S. Rule applies to not only those dead woodchucks you are assigned to support but also to many other situations where being candid can build credibility for the content and set proper expectations for learners. This is important in motivating employees to keep trying new skills on the job until they have mastered them.

The problem is that training programs often tout a supposedly perfect process to deal with a situation. Then when learners go back and try a new skill and for whatever reason it doesn't work as advertised, they blame the process and promptly abandon it. Setting realistic expectations can help employees continue trying what you have taught them.

For example, in a maintenance situation, you might need to say, "It turns out, for this problem our Incidence of Repair statistics aren't going to be of much help. The most frequent fix has only worked in 15% of the cases, so we're still trying to get our arms around what's going wrong. That's why you need to be sure to report your own fix when you encounter this. We need more repair data."

Or you may have to tell service reps, "This conflict management process is designed to help you calm someone down. It works on an emotional level, but it isn't guaranteed to work when the customer is asking for something we can't give. In those cases, the best you can do is stay calm yourself, listen carefully, offer alternatives where you can, and pass the customer up the line to your supervisor if that isn't enough. Some people just aren't going to calm down no matter what you do. But that doesn't mean you shouldn't use the conflict management process anyway."

In general, if your learners are thinking it, then you need to acknowledge it, especially if their attitude going in might be negative. If there are any weaknesses in your training, then you need to address them openly. Otherwise, learners will abandon what you've taught them the minute they get into trouble with it.

This is hard for management to accept, but it is essential in order to get the biggest payback from training. A little bit of candor up front can generate big benefits back on the job.

○ To Do

You can't ignore the emotional component to training design. If there is some initial skepticism, then you need to deal with it.

1. Expand your needs analysis to include any relevant history with similar training topics. If you are relatively new, this may mean checking with some long-time employees.
2. Include a discussion of the emotional reaction to the content being presented. Is there a proverbial elephant in the room that will undermine this content if it is ignored?
3. Decide what the message should be to create early nod momentum with learners. What do they need to hear to quickly connect with the training and be eager to hear what comes next?
4. Make sure that management understands what a Home On the Range attitude does to learning results and why a candid approach pays back big-time when there are emotional issues. Leaders need to understand that you aren't insulting past practices; you're addressing natural employee concerns about the new content.

The No B.S. Rule is all about your credibility. Management lives in a political world, where hiding mistakes may be the norm, whereas you live in the performance world, where results are what counts. Being candid with learners will help drive those results.

The Penalty of Seductive Content

HERE IS A SIMPLE QUESTION:

- Group A received training on the principles of electricity.
- Group B received the same training on electricity, and the content was supplemented by an interesting story of what happens when someone is struck by lightning that illustrated those principles.

So which group scored higher on post-training tests?

As you can imagine, everyone selects Group B—the students who heard the story. But the answer is, *Group A scored higher!*[1]

No question, Group B liked the training better on the basis of the post-training "smile sheets"—Kirkpatrick Level 1 evaluation. But that isn't what we asked. The question was which group tested higher for knowledge—Kirkpatrick Level 2 evaluation. And that was definitely Group A, the training *without* the story. How can this be? It's the total opposite of what most people assume should happen.

To understand, you need to think back to Chapter 3.1 and the concept of cognitive load. The message there is that students have a limited capacity for learning. This capacity is affected by the complexity of the material, how it is taught, and what other extraneous elements are present. The goal of a designer is to simplify the content and weed out the unnecessary elements in order to free up as much instruction load capacity as possible.

What happened here is that the story added for Group B actually created unnecessary load. This is what researchers call *seductive content,* material that is emotionally satisfying for both the instructor and the student, yet that actually reduces learning.

That is exactly what occurred in the electricity study. Everyone enjoyed the example, but it created more "stuff" for learners to pay attention to. The additional content interfered with the fundamental electricity principles being taught.

This is a long-established principle in instructional design that many trainers fail to consider. Typical research comments are as follows:

"Since the late 1980s we've known about the harmful effects of interesting tidbits added to lessons to stimulate emotional interest ... Because of their harmful effects on learning, these types of additions are called *seductive details*."[2,3]

"Evidence shows that adding motivational content—even content topically related to the lesson—depresses learning."[4]

And it's important to note that seductive content is not just about the training itself. It also applies to associated visuals.

"Not only did the interesting (but irrelevant) visuals not improve learning—they actually disrupted the formation of the desired mental models and depressed learning!"[5]

Although learners certainly appreciate being entertained, what they really want is to minimize training time. "Tell me what I need to know, and then shut up and let me leave" is their attitude. This is a hard message for trainers to accept.

Yet the research is clear that many of those things we love to do, and that make students love us, actually *depress* learning. For classroom training, that can include the topical humor, great stories, clever asides, and perfect analogies that we have honed over the years. For e-learning, it can include the stunning backgrounds, music clips, funny sounds, beautiful pictures, and detailed animations. It's heartbreaking to have to toss out these supposed training gems, but it's a necessity.

To understand why these elements have to go, it's important to understand why they are included in the first place.

The main reason training contains so much seductive content is because *the training is too long.* Instructional designers use seductive content in an attempt to counteract massive violations of adult attention span constraints. Another reason is that training is often *too boring,* like screen-flipping e-learning. The combination of length and boredom is coma inducing, so seductive content becomes the tool to counter them.

We talked in Chapter 3.3 about the realities of attention and that you only have about 5 to 15 minutes to work with. Because most training lasts for hours and days, course authors must use gimmicks in an attempt to maintain student concentration (or consciousness) over time. So you get all this seductive content along with needless activities thrown in to break up long teaching sequences. The result is reduced learning.

It's inescapable. The more unnecessary load you put into your training programs, the less instruction load capacity students have to actually learn something. And the more seductive content you include, the more it will interfere with the real content you want them to learn.

◗ To Do

This is a Terrible Too issue that we're going to keep pounding away on. Seductive content is a mistake necessitated by creating courses that are too long and too boring.

1. You have 5 to 15 minutes at a time to work with. Accept it once and for all and move on.
2. Be alert to seductive content warning signs. You may catch yourself saying:
    "We need something to break this up here."
    "They'll enjoy this."
    "We need to get them moving and doing something about now."
    "This would be funny."
3. Prepare yourself emotionally to let go of things you may love to do but that don't necessarily move the core content along. Remember, employees want you to teach them what they need to know as quickly as possible and then shut up.

4. Put all your course material through a seductive content evaluation. Is this teaching the content? Is it building understanding? Or is it interfering with retention by needlessly giving learners more to think about? Is it just trying to keep people awake or to get higher ratings on the smile sheets?
5. Be merciless about cutting seductive content. We know, these bits are your pride and joy and they make your training life worth living, but they have to go.

You like to do it. Learners like to experience it. That's why it is so seductive. Get rid of it, and watch your learning results improve.

Eliminate Split Attention

AS LONG AS WE ARE TALKING about common instructional design practices that actually depress learning, here's another one—with a ready example:

A Virginia Tech study of truck drivers found that texting while driving increased the collision risk by 23 times versus non-distracted driving. Amazingly, this is even higher than the danger of driving at the legally drunk limit, which is seven times more risky.[1]

The factor at play here is something called *split attention.* Whether it's doing a job as important as driving safely or completing more mundane tasks such as training, it's clear that people are not good at paying attention to more than one thing at a time.

We know from Part 3 that learners have limited capacities when it comes to cognitive load, attention span, and short-term memory. Overload any of these and learning performance suffers, just like with texting while driving. Using our research terms, split attention generates unnecessary cognitive load.

A good example of split attention in training is the rapid-development software that converts existing *PowerPoint* files to click-and-read e-learning. The output is typically a multi-window program containing slides, an animated slide title list for navigation, and audio narration or a talking-head video. Some programs also provide additional window sections containing a scrolling full-text version of the audio track or additional source content supporting the slides.

The result is that there can be as many as six different inputs to the visual sketchpad subsystem of working memory, as well as multiple inputs to the audio loop subsystem. Slides are animating and advancing, titles are highlighting in sequence, a face is talking, and text may be scrolling. There's a forced split in attention. So where do learners focus their eyes and ears?

The answer is that students spend a lot of mental effort trying to figure that out for themselves, which reduces their learning results. Research has shown that split attention factors can depress learning by as much as 50%.[2]

Here's a summary of the general rules for minimizing split attention in learning:[3-5]

- Study in a quiet environment. It leads to better learning. This means no phone, radio, iPod, TV, or other PC applications.
- In general, study alone. The fewer potential distractions, the better.
- Present content in as few modes as possible to make it understandable.
- Take advantage of the independent functioning of the visual sketchpad and auditory loop components of working memory. For example, a graphic with an audio explanation (different modes) is more effective than a graphic with a text explanation (same mode).
- Use specific techniques to draw attention to important parts of content. This includes arrows and lines for complex graphics, color, font variations and formatting for text, and vocal emphasis for narration.
- Present related content in a single medium. Switching back and forth—such as between a computer screen and a manual—needlessly eats up learning capacity by forcing students to integrate the two.
- Within a single medium, present related visual content near to each other. They should not be separated on a page or screen or on different pages or windows.
- With video, when a presenter is shown, integrate the presenter with the content in a single window. Much like an evening news weatherperson, the presenter can then direct the learner's attention

by visual cues such as talking into the camera ("Look at me") and turning to point at content or even going offscreen ("Look at this").
- Leave out unnecessary text, visuals, animations, and sounds.
- Eliminate redundant content in different delivery modes, such as narrating on-screen text word for word or adding text to self-explanatory graphics.
- Follow these same content integration principles in the design of external performance aids.

As an instructional designer, you have to assist learners in focusing their attention on the important elements of your content. This is especially critical for novice learners and for complex material generating a large content cognitive load.

◯ To Do

In order to maximize results, you need to carefully manage learner attention.

1. Analyze your current program development tools for elements of split attention. How much is going on at once? Is the program competing with itself for attention? Do learners always know where they are supposed to be looking?
2. Select and use tools that provide a single attention source.
3. When it's absolutely necessary to use click-and-read *PowerPoint* conversion tools, minimize the number of windows offered.

Attention is a precious commodity in learning. Trainers need to help students focus solely on the point being taught and not confuse learners with a variety of elements competing with each other.

Engagement to Interaction

WE WERE SITTING IN A MEETING with the head of training, his boss, an end-user executive, and several other consultants. The discussion concerned problems with the remote handheld network used during live satellite TV training broadcasts. The PC-based hardware for signing on and participating in the courses was not working. Everybody hated the system, including the students, who were happy when it was down because they didn't want to be called on during national broadcasts.

The end-user executive finally asked, "Why do we even need these stupid handhelds? Why can't we just watch the programs?"

The training director had invested a lot of time and money in the system, and his reputation was at stake. He turned to his media consultant, a professor from a major Midwestern university, and asked, "Tell them why we need interactivity."

You could see the emotions playing over the consultant's face. He was clearly thinking, "Do I or don't I?" He finally came to a decision and said, "Actually, it's not the physical interaction that matters. Research shows that it's mental engagement that drives learning." That didn't make the training director happy, but it was the right answer.

Think of TV game shows such as *Jeopardy!, Wheel of Fortune, The Price is Right, Password, Family Feud, Cash Cab*, and even the simple *Deal or No Deal* guessing game. What's the secret to their popularity?

Even though broadcast TV is supposedly a passive medium, viewers watch these programs because they enjoy playing along mentally at home. They don't have to be clicking a button to be fully engaged. They are shouting out answers or advice at the TV. There's an important lesson here.

This is a little-known learning factor that has enormous implications for trainers, especially for designers of e-learning. Organizations spend lots of money on a learn/practice model where practice consists of solving problems and answering questions about the content. Learning is assumed to require regular mouse-click interactions or actual testing, and significant development time and money are spent providing them. Yet research indicates that these are not resources well spent.

Here's a sample of what experts say about the power of mental engagement compared with physical interaction:

"There were no significant differences in learning between active and passive groups."[1]

"It's not the format of the question that is important; rather, it's the mental process that the question stimulates ... Overt activity may not always result in better learning or greater satisfaction among learners."[2]

"As long as learners are requested to respond to inserted questions, generally similar benefits of questioning are obtained whether the responses are overt or covert or whether the material is preceded or followed by the questions."[3]

In fact, physical interactivity can actually *depress* learning because it increases the cognitive load on learners:

"Conventional models of instruction in many domains involve the presentation of a principle, concept, or rule, followed by extensive practice on problems applying the rule. This approach at first glance seems like commonsense—providing ample skills practice is 'learning by doing.' However, cognitive load theory suggests that such instructional approaches may actually be hurting learners' understanding of the subject matter."[4]

"If a behavioral activity included in a lesson adds too much extraneous cognitive load, it may defeat its purpose. … In some situations, behavioral activity can take more time and result in less learning."[5]

The research is clear that it's not about the questioning method—mouse-click or paper test versus mental engagement. The critical factor in learner involvement is *instructional design.*

"Well-designed multimedia instructional messages can promote active cognitive processing in students, even when learners seem to be behaviorally inactive."[6]

Asking students a question, giving them time to determine an answer, and then immediately providing them with the correct response is just as powerful when it is posed within the content as when it requires a mouse click on a button or a circled answer on a test.

For example, a so-called passive medium such as digital video, designed with elements of mental engagement, is fully capable of driving the required cognitive processing needed for efficient learning and retention.

"There is a pervasive belief, increasingly being challenged by research, that television and video viewing is a passive activity in which viewers are only superficially reactive to what they are watching, and one that will, over time, hamper or displace academic achievement. However, recent studies support the theory that viewing is instead an active process, one which can be 'an ongoing and highly interconnected process of monitoring and comprehending' and 'a complex, cognitive activity that develops and matures with the child's development to promote learning.'"[7]

That said, there are also new learner preferences to deal with. Just a few years ago, streaming passive video to a handheld device was revolutionary. Today, users can play full-function video games and run complex applications such as photo manipulation and video editing.

The expectation now is that learning should be an interactive exercise. End-users want to have control over their experience rather than simply sit and watch. Regardless of the research, this has to be taken into account.

Clearly, the idea that learners must physically do something with new content in the form of some sort of formal interaction is a false assumption. Properly designed *mental engagement* course structures allow students to "play along at home" and get the same learning benefits as with physical interaction. But whether the interactive is active or passive, the critical factor is still proper instructional design.

◯ To Do

It's not about the way questions are asked. It's about the mental engagement the questions create.

1. Familiarize yourself with the research on engagement. You are going to need your proof sources.
2. This challenges a long-held assumption by trainers, so you are going to experience some push-back. It will take some convincing, but the research is the research. Don't try to win this battle in the first conversation. Work on it over time.
3. Focus on the business case for using the power of engagement design elements. This opens up media such as audio and video to be full-fledged options for learning, which can dramatically reduce development costs, shorten deployment cycle time, reduce student contact time, and increase learner satisfaction.
4. Select a pilot project and implement the practice portion of it using mental engagement activities. On the basis of the results, consider standardizing on this approach.

Many organizations now deliver *all* their training using online media such as video with embedded mental and physical engagement exercises. This provides strategic and tactical advantages for the organization and simplifies the life of trainers. It also opens up e-learning to mobile delivery platforms where physical interaction may be limited.

PowerPoint ≠ Notes

WE HAVE ALL HAD THE LAMENTABLE EXPERIENCE of sitting through a lengthy death-by-*PowerPoint* session consisting of an endless string of slides loaded with information. Rousing ourselves back to consciousness at the end, we've wondered what causes presenters to think that this is an effective way to communicate with people and that slides like these help in any way.

It turns out that the root cause of many problems with slide-based programs is actually the instructional designer's approach toward *note-taking*. Yes, note-taking. Here is what is happening.

A subject matter expert (SME) creates a slide presentation. The SME is not an instructional designer, so the slide set focuses on content and has two purposes. The first is to guide the trainer through what is to be presented. The second is to totally document the content because the student materials most often consist of a printout of the slides. That printout may leave room for note-taking, such as a 3-up format with space on the right, or have minimal room for notes such as a full-page or 6-up format.

As a result, slides are loaded with content and are text heavy. They have to be because the slides themselves are the only official record of what is said during the presentation. Certainly, some presentations may have additional text available on a Notes page printout, but this *PowerPoint* feature is rarely used because it creates extra work for the SME—often more effort than authoring the slides themselves requires in the first place.

Every communications tutorial talks about making slides highly visual and using only short phrases of text. But this means that trainers need something else to prompt them through their presentation. And learners are required to do extensive note-taking if they are to have any record of the actual content.

Those are the two choices for SMEs. Load the slides up with everything there is to say, or net them out and hope that trainers are properly qualified and that learners take good notes. It isn't a very good set of options. Although SMEs and course authors may not like it, the research is clear on this subject:

> *Slides and student materials should be separate documents, and note-taking should be minimized.*

You can't use the program slides or screens as the course documentation that learners take away with them. It creates ineffective slides. You also can't have learners taking notes. It lowers their learning. Here's the research as to what is going on.

Cognitive overload.

Note-taking creates extreme mental demands on learners and can overload working memory. In addition to listening for comprehension, learners have to deal with the analysis of content, identification of important points, and formulating and recording of notes. In fact, the act of note-taking requires more cognitive effort than playing chess, reading a book, or memorizing a list of nonsense syllables.[1]

Lost information.

Note-taking creates a split attention situation.[2] Learners have to listen to a 150 words per minute presentation while writing notes at about 25 words per minute—all in real time. They can't simultaneously do both effectively, so they quickly fall behind. As a result, they either miss something that's presented or they fail to document an important point for later reference.

Wrong information.
Many learners don't know how to maintain accurate notes.[3] Because they're learning the content for the first time, they have trouble identifying the important parts of it. They write too much or too little. They capture incorrect information. They don't store notes in an orderly fashion for easy retrieval later. They rely on recording technology to capture everything, but then they don't condense and review the media files for the highlights.[4]

Not effective.
Contrary to common assumptions, the act of note-taking does not necessarily help learning. In one study, learners were asked to write two essays, one immediately after a lecture and the other one week later, both without referring to their notes. The essays of the learners who took notes were no better than the learners who just listened.[5]

Here is additional research supporting the separation of student notes from course screens and slides.

Slides should be succinct.
Individual screens or slides should address a single point and contain a minimum amount of text—ideally five words or fewer per point.[6] That way learners can focus on the visual elements and the auditory information. This means that detailed information must reside elsewhere.

Prepared notes are effective.
In the study mentioned earlier, all learners listened to a lecture without taking notes. They were then asked to write an essay one week later. Some learners were given notes prepared by the trainer, and the others had no notes. The learners with the prepared notes wrote better essays than the learners without notes.[7]

Hand notes out at the end.
Another learning point of the prepared notes study is when to distribute notes. Handing out notes at the beginning of a program just

gives learners something else to distract them. We've all seen this in watching attendees leafing ahead in the student binder during class.

This is why some trainers prefer to hand out notes to attendees at the end of the program. Their general rule is to never put information in front of learners that they aren't going to immediately use. This helps learners devote their full attention to the training.

To summarize:
- The act of taking notes reduces learning.
- The notes students take may not be accurate or on point.
- The act of note-taking is not what elevates learning. It's having notes available to reference when studying.
- Who created the notes is not critical. What's important is how good the notes are. In practice, it's safe to assume that SME-prepared notes are likely to be more comprehensive than learner notes created in-session.

For SMEs and course developers, the message is clear. Copying slides or screens is not the right approach for documenting the content of programs. Deliverables should consist of the content along with suitable student notes already prepared for learners. The notes don't need to be 100% complete. It's certainly acceptable to have students take a few notes, particularly when the instructor is cuing them on what the important content is.

It may also be necessary to create leader notes. If done properly, student notes can provide sufficient cues for the presenter so that only one set of notes is necessary.

The result is a more interesting set of slides or screens, as well as a more attentive audience that is guaranteed to leave with an effective set of notes.

◐ To Do

There is no denying it. This is going to take additional work to do it right.

1. Share this research so that everyone understands the penalty of loading slides and screens up with textual content.
2. Convince SMEs and developers that they have to abandon the expectation that learners can take their own notes as needed.
3. Build the creation of separate slides and prepared student notes into your standard processes.
4. Make slides and screens visually effective, and leave the details for the notes.

There is no reason to let the lack of notes force you into creating boring or overwhelming visuals or slides. Separate the two and watch the effectiveness of your programs improve, and see your student satisfaction ratings soar.

4.8

Practice May Not Make Perfect

WHETHER IT'S FOR A COMPLEX WORKPLACE TASK or a simple athletic skill, the classic teaching process uses a simple four-step cycle:

Tell   = explanation
Show = example
Try   = practice
Coach = feedback

For example, using this model, how would you teach a young child to field a ground ball? It might go something like this.

"OK, get down into a gorilla crouch and hang your hands down, like this. Make sure your glove is touching the dirt. (Tell) Now, roll a ball to me. See how I stopped it with my glove and then put my other hand over the ball? (Show) Now, get in the gorilla position and I'll roll a ball to you. (Try … ball rolls under the glove) Good try. See what happened? Your glove wasn't in the dirt. (Coach) Let's try it again with your glove all the way down. (Try … ball goes into glove.) Good stop!"

Training programs should consist of a series of these cycles covering the individual points of the content. In the classic training process, the Tell and Show steps take up about two-thirds of the contact time, with Try and Coach steps taking up the remaining one-third.

Most trainers agree that practice is an integral part of any training program. Practice allows learners to not only try what they have just been taught but also use practice exercises to provide additional content (discovery learning) and to develop further insights into the content.

Yet this Try step delivers both good and bad news. The good news is that practice helps with mastery. The bad news is that practice can significantly increase cognitive load and potentially overload working memory, actually *depressing* learning. Fortunately, research indicates that there are several ways to deal with this.

Worked examples.

A worked example is a step-by-step demonstration of how to perform a process, similar to a math teacher walking the class through an algebra problem. A worked example allows learners to build a mental model of how to complete a process rather than having to figure it out for themselves.

Replacing some practice with worked examples has definite benefits. Studies have reported an overall reduction in training time and testing time required, along with fewer training and testing errors through the greater use of worked examples.[1]

Think of all those math courses you took growing up. Class usually consisted of an example, followed by an assignment of extensive homework for practice. Have you ever completed a group of problems and then by final exam time forgotten how you did them? Solving the homework problems took up so much working memory capacity that there was little left for the learning itself. The goal became finishing your assignment versus learning the mathematical principles. Worked examples addresses this.

Hybrid examples/practice.

A question that arises is how to transition from full worked examples to full practice. One approach is to utilize a hybrid combination of examples and practice called *completion examples.* Here some of the steps of a process are taught as a worked example, and one or more of the steps are left for the learner to solve. This considerably reduces the scope of a learner's practice requirement and keeps the learner's cognitive load within acceptable limits.[2]

Backward fading.

A specialized form of completion example is *backward fading*. This is the process of gradually increasing the number of steps learners must complete on their own, starting with the last step and working backward until the learner is performing the complete process.

This allows learners to master a process gradually, always focusing on the overall result. As they develop their skills, they do more and more work. Although the benefit appears to be small, this can improve learning versus having worked examples go straight from initial problem to solution.[3]

Self-explanation engagements.

Another method that can moderately improve learning is the use of *self-explanation questions*.[4] Instead of going from big-picture concepts to process step details, this approach does the reverse. Learners see a worked example and then answer questions about the concepts behind the solution. This helps them make the link between fundamentals and specific processes.

Hints.

Regardless of your method of Show and Try, you can always increase mental engagement by providing learners with hints. You can provide helpful comments during engagement activities, or you can eliminate options during multiple-choice questions. Just make sure to always explain your reasoning so that there is a learning point taught with each hint.

NOTE! Research shows that worked examples are more effective for novice learners than for experts.[5] As learners begin to master skills, an all-problems approach is more efficient. For experts, worked examples actually depress learning.

So straight practice is not always the most efficient way to train employees. To maximize learning and minimize training time for new learners, the Show component of a course should begin with worked examples. Then the Try component should consist of a series of completion examples, which could optionally use backward fading. Then the training or post-training can end with full problem practice. This will help novice learners master content in a way that controls their cognitive load.

◗ **To Do**
To learn more about the science of worked examples, we recommend you read *Efficiency in Learning: Evidence-Based Guidelines to Manage Cognitive Load* by Ruth Colvin Clark, Frank Nguyen, and John Sweller (Pfeiffer, 2006).

Authoring effective examples and creating proper practice engagements is as important as the structure behind the teaching itself. Yet instructional designers typically spend most of their attention on Tell issues and not as much on Show and Try, which is what drives the ultimate payoff in business results.

A Few More Tips ...

A FEW MORE BITS of instructional design research are worth mentioning because trainers often miss them. These tips are definitely useful, but they don't require a whole chapter to explain. They're listed in the general flow of the functions in a training program (the backbone!)

One thing at a time.
We've discussed the realities of attention span and cognitive load. The bottom line is "shorter is better," where "short" is defined at 5 to 15 minutes. This means that more complex content has to be chunked up into digestible segments.

In general, it's better to have two 10-minute programs each covering one concept than one 20-minute program covering two concepts. This segmenting helps maximize teaching cognitive load capacity. For example, our Key Account Selling program, formerly a 2½ day classroom training course, now consists of 35 video-based e-learning programs averaging about 12 minutes in length each. Total contact time is significantly reduced, and actual learning is increased.

A rapid pace is better.
There is a Goldilocks nature to the pace of learning. It should be neither too fast nor too slow. It needs to be just right.

In general, a relatively rapid pace leads to better learning.[1] The pace needs to be brisk and energizing, but not so fast that learners struggle to keep up. Pace may also need to be slower for novice learners or for complex content. There is no specific guideline for pace. It requires piloting programs and observing learners.

Use conversational language.

With many programs, on-screen text is narrated and video is presented from a teleprompter. This creates a number of problems.

First, writing for the ear is very different than writing for the eye. What seems normal as read usually comes off stilted when spoken. (That's why speechwriters have a very different skill set than authors.)

Second, most presenters lose their natural vocal rhythm and inflection when speaking from a script. Coming across as natural is a professional level media skill.

Third, media pros can actually be too smooth, which hurts the credibility of the content. The result is that programs often come across as a "pitch" versus training.

Research shows that conversational language is more effective than formal language in training programs.[2] This means developers must either be effective scriptwriters or use technology to record natural-sounding presentations and turn them into scripts. It also means that narration or video scripts need to use straightforward language rather than a fancy vocabulary. This makes programs much more accessible to learners.

Omit unnecessary audio.

e-Learning programs will often include background music or sounds to punch up a course. There is extensive research showing that this significantly depresses learning. For example, in one study students taking a course that removed music and environmental sounds had an average gain in learning of 105%.[3]

Omit unnecessary graphics and words.

Instructional designers will often insert interesting but unrelated graphics into programs in order to visually dress up the slides or screens. A number of studies have found that this reduces learning, even with young adults raised on high production value media.[4]

The same is true for extraneous words added for interest.[5] In general, any unnecessary content depresses learning because it adds to cognitive load and can cause split attention.

Animations are not necessarily better.

A common design assumption is that providing content in a more visually appealing style such as animations improves learning. This can be an extra development expense that is not necessarily justified. A number of studies have found that there is no difference in effectiveness between static graphics or animations.[6]

The thinking now in instructional design is that the choice of visual representation style should reflect the structure of content itself. Use animations when they provide unique contributions to understanding the content.

Minimize the use of links in e-learning.

Creating links leading to other instructional material generally lowers learning.[7] As many as half of learners see a link and assume it leads to supplemental content, so they bypass it. Many students who select the link abandon it before completion and prematurely return to the main program sequence. Either way, key content goes untaught.

Structure engagement activities properly.

Test sections are commonly used to break up boring stretches of content. It's well-established that paced practice is more effective than mass practice.[8] This is why you need to distribute engagement activities throughout a program rather than bunching them up.

Then make sure that these engagements require learners to apply content rather than simply to regurgitate what has just been taught. Your goal is to help learners integrate new information into memory rather than to merely spit it back at you.

Finally, be sure to provide explanatory feedback after an engagement.[9] The most powerful learning situation is to take a test and have it graded immediately thereafter. Also, remember to discuss the incorrect answers and why they're wrong. That way you create multiple learning points from a single question.

Include tips/heads-ups/gotchas.

For any training topic, there is the book-learning portion of the content. This is typically the focus of most training programs. But there is also a street-smarts component to be gained from the SME's experience.

In addition to the content itself, students want the benefit of the SME's additional insight into the practicalities of using the skills. They want to know about any tips the SME has gleaned from experience. They want to be alerted to issues that may crop up. They want to be warned about common mistakes that novices tend to make. In our experience, this is one of the highest rated portions of training programs because it delivers real-world information.

Quit depending on smile sheets.

Student post-course satisfaction surveys (Kirkpatrick Level 1) are not valid indicators of training effectiveness. For example, a study of student course ratings versus test results for 1,200 employees found that there was no correlation between the ratings and actual learning.[10]

In addition, students are not professional educators and they aren't trained on how to accurately grade the instructional effectiveness of a program. If you want to evaluate a course, determine its quality for yourself. Get in there and watch it. Then track business results from the training.

Don't make tests too hard.

Everyone suffers from test anxiety to some extent, and few people enjoy tests. We've seen organizations where employees were too worried to learn because they knew a make-or-break test was coming at the end of the course. So the test was actually counterproductive. It depressed learning even as it tried to provide a motivation to learn.

Our philosophy is that testing should document successful completion of the course. After all, it's only a Kirkpatrick Level 2 knowledge measure, not a Level 4 results measure. We write our tests so that they are relatively easy to pass if you've taken the course and hard to guess your way through if you haven't. That way the test is not a hurdle to learning. It simply documents completion for performance management and compliance record keeping.

▷ To Do

If you want to learn more about instructional design, we highly recommend you read *Building Expertise: Cognitive Methods for Training and Performance Improvement*, 3rd. Ed. by Ruth Colvin Clark (Pfeiffer, 2008).

Part 5

How to Deliver Effective Training

SO FAR, WE'VE FOCUSED OUR ATTENTION on the conceptual ground rules for effective training. This is important "know" information, but it's time now to examine the "do" messages that these principles support.

In this Part 5, we analyze the various methods of delivering training, from classic big meetings to the most advanced multimedia approaches. Questions that need to be addressed include:

What's the role for e-learning?
Does it make sense to continue holding big meetings?
What are the various pros and cons for different
*   e-learning methods?*
How can we make webinars better?
What should we do about mobile learning?
Where does video fit in?

The Airtight Case for e-Learning

IF RIP VAN WINKLE WOKE UP TODAY, one industry he'd recognize is training. For most organizations, the bulk of employee development is still classroom based.[1] The average training model is little different than the traditional one-room schoolhouse in *Little House on the Prairie.* It is a "sage on the stage" presentation to a mixed-experience group of workers. Concepts are taught, and then practice problems are completed.

Even the use of computers has had minimal impact in many organizations. The Internet has made research easier (even as it has made validating that research tougher). And the use of e-learning has been very rudimentary, with the bulk of it violating much of the research we discussed in Parts 3 and 4.

So it is no wonder that trainers, when discussing e-learning, ask the question, "So how much do you lose in moving a classroom course to e-learning?" The built-in assumption is that e-learning can't deliver the effectiveness of in-person teaching. This seems commonsense, but it's the wrong question.

The fact is that research since the early 1990s has indicated that e-learning consistently delivers *better* results than traditional learning.[2] Reported benefits of e-learning have included the following:
- 60% faster learning curve
- 50% higher retention
- 56% greater gains in learning
- 40% higher consistency of presentation

- 60% increase in consistency of learning
- Training compression of 70%

Yet for years, educators started with the standard "e-learning is inferior" premise. Now there are two major meta-studies (a study of studies) that show otherwise.

A 2003 *International Review of Research in Open and Distance Learning* report analyzed 86 face-to-face (F2F) versus distance education (DE) studies covering 15,000 students. In the discussion section, it made the following observation about the "inferior" assumption:

> "This analysis demonstrates that students engaged in DE academically outperform their F2F counterparts. We have been focusing all along on the question: 'Is DE suitable for all students?' The results of this study may raise the inverse question: 'Is F2F suitable for all students?' and may begin a paradigm shift in the way postsecondary education is pedagogically conceptualized."[3]

So rather than reducing student performance, this meta-study found that e-learning *outperforms* classroom learning—just the opposite of the traditional assumption.

The definitive research on this question was published by the U.S. Department of Education in 2009. This was the final nail in the coffin of the "e-learning is inferior" position:

> "A systematic search of the research literature from 1996 through July 2008 identified more than a thousand empirical studies of online learning. Analysts screened these studies to find those that (a) contrasted an online to a face-to-face condition, (b) measured student learning outcomes, (c) used a rigorous research design, and (d) provided adequate information to calculate an effect size. As a result of this screening, 51 independent effects were identified that could be subjected to meta-analysis. *The meta-analysis found that, on average, students in online learning conditions performed better than those receiving face-to-face instruction.*"[4]

You can see the results of this research in the gradual shift in higher education offerings. More than 6,000 online degrees are now offered by nearly 400 accredited schools.[5] In addition, there are over 140 accredited online high school degree programs currently available.[6] And these numbers are increasing.

All this comes as a major surprise to most business professionals, but the research is conclusive. e-Learning actually *outperforms* the traditional classroom learning experience. It's not that there is anything inherently wrong with the classroom. Indeed, some learning applications can require it. It's that a classroom structure creates Terrible Too's that e-learning avoids:

- Classroom training is too long. It exceeds adult attention span limits and creates overwhelming cognitive load.
- The large amount of information being taught interferes with itself, so there is reduced retention.
- Classes contain seductive details in an attempt to maintain learner attention. This lowers learning by adding unnecessary content.
- It's not economically feasible to bring employees together for short segments of training.
- It's not economically feasible to provide training to any employee who wants it or needs it.
- It's not economically feasible to have different training programs for novices versus experienced employees. One size has to fit all.
- Employees have to be taken off the job to learn. Assembling multiple employees in one spot creates lost time, whether it's traveling to a remote seminar or going back and forth to the training room on campus.
- Much of classroom training is anticipation learning, with a significant delay between the event and the application of the content.
- Classroom training is a one-and-done event. There is no facility for refresh learning or for new hires who come on board after the training event.
- Classroom training is inconsistent. Individual instructors have different levels of teaching skills. Compliance with the instructional design can vary from course to course—even with the

same presenter. And even when the course agenda is adhered to, attendee questions introduce different learning points from class to class.

In contrast, e-learning is a better fit for the requirements of adult learners and the realities of today's workplace:
- Individual programs can be as short as needed.
- Programs can cover a single learning point.
- Different versions of training can be created for novice and experienced learners, or refresh learners can easily skim the content in a non-linear fashion.
- All unnecessary content can be removed.
- Training time is reduced by 40% to 60% of classroom training time.[7]
- Training can be delivered at any time to any employee, repeatedly, and at a negligible marginal cost.
- Training can be delivered on the job on mobile devices.
- Training can be delivered just as needed with no delay between learning and use of the new skills.
- Every learner can receive the exact same course experience, every time.

If you could provide classroom training on demand, in the workplace, with proper instructional design, and deliver it consistently in 10-minute blocks, classroom would perform just as well as e-learning (although it would still be more expensive). But that isn't the case. Whether it's a series of one-hour courses in a school day or a multi-day employee training seminar, classroom learning can't meet those requirements. Consequently, it doesn't generate the same business results.

◗ **To Do**

If you're still in the "e-learning is inferior" camp, then you need to get up to speed on the latest research.

1. Download the IRRODL and DOE reports referenced earlier. The DOE report in particular is a must-read for trainers.
2. Be realistic about the actual effects of classroom learning and what research has to say about it.
3. We talked in Part 1 about understanding the complete costs of training. Start analyzing the total costs of classroom training in your organization, and see what the potential savings would be in placing a greater emphasis on an e-learning model.

Most organizations are slowly converting to e-learning, primarily in the compliance areas, where their main goal is to certify employee completion of the courses. Tremendous gains can be obtained from speeding up that conversion into all areas of training.

5.2

A Rant on Big Meetings

A SPECIAL CASE OF THE CLASSROOM EXPERIENCE is a standard ritual in organizations—the "big meeting." Even though we just pounded on the classroom issue, the big meeting phenomenon is so painful that it merits its own rant. The following story should sound familiar.

A front-line marketing specialist attended the annual 2-day sales extravaganza that everyone hated. The meeting consisted of a steady stream of product manager presentations for full 8-hour days, with a 15-minute break in the morning and afternoon.

She and her buddies were trying to guess how many slides they were going to see, so she decided to bring an attendance clicker and count them (with money changing hands based on the total). The result for the two days was *over 700 slides*. And these weren't simple slides. They were chock full of pictures and charts and heavy with specifications and statistics.

She said that it was like the old joke about why you can't teach pigs to sing—a pig can't sing in the first place, and it irritates the pig. She was saying that there was no way the attendees could absorb all that content, and they were definitely unhappy afterwards at being put through the experience.

Management is relentless in designing ridiculously killer meetings. You hear this attitude all the time in comments like these leading up to a big event:

"Let's plan on having a working lunch."

"As long as they're here, we should work them."

"We need to keep them until 6:00 p.m."

"We have to add three more presentations somewhere."

"If it's important to them, they'll remember it."

"We shouldn't have to spoon feed them. It's their job."

"We can only tell them what they need to know. We can't make them learn it."

It's no wonder attendees always say that the highlight of meetings is trading stories with their peers afterwards in the bar. Events like these become poster children for every bad thing we talked about in the previous chapter. Let the rant begin.

Too long.

Let us see if we have this right. You give attendees one 15-minute break in a 4-hour morning. You overload their stomachs with a heavy lunch. Then you give them a single 15-minute break in a 4-hour afternoon. And this is assuming that you don't keep them past 5:00 p.m. because the presentations ran long and you have to get caught up. Then you do it again tomorrow. Is that how it goes? Are you kidding?

To review, we all have between 5 and 15 minutes of attention span. So basically, everything after 8:15 a.m. is getting something less than full attention. Even if we assume that attention span restarts after every break, you're probably getting less than an hour of full attention per each 8-hour day.

Too much.

Nothing quite compares with taking active professionals who are used to moving around, talking, meeting, and working on a fast-changing variety of projects and making them sit for 16 hours over two days.

This is not drinking from a fire hose. It's making a snowball in the middle of an avalanche. You're not talking about cognitive overload here. You're talking about cognitive "numb-nification"—that out-of-body feeling at the end of a long meeting day where you're happy just to have survived the experience.

Big meetings give no thought whatsoever to how much learners can actually absorb. These are primeval "see" events where the goal is to make certain all the required content is flashed past attendees' eyeballs. Once the photons have hit the optic nerves and their eardrums have been vibrated, management doesn't care what happens after that. "Are they here and are they awake?" is all that counts.

The entire meeting is one big interference event, where the next pitch happily overlays what went before it. Then you're so tired by the last pitch that you don't remember much of it, either. So the end result is that attendees remember nothing.

Too hard.

Most of the presentations individually are too complex and generate massive cognitive overload. They are not only too long for maintaining attention but also typically include a classic *PowerPoint* death march with every slide a master's thesis.

Poor presenters.

Don't get us started on the typical quality of the presentations themselves. We're not talking about motivational speakers here. We're talking about SMEs who have an abiding and deep love for their content and want the captive attendees to share in their depth of knowledge and affection for the topic.

Or we're talking about presenters who have been assigned to give this pitch and are frantic to get through it without tripping up. Add to this the specter of dry content, and you have a vision of Ben Stein's political science class in *Ferris Bueller's Day Off* with drool on the desk and all … only it's not for just a 50-minute school period. It's for 16 hours.

Slides for notes.

Chapter 4.7 explained why printing out presentation slides is a poor substitute for notes. They are not good notes, and the act of note-taking lowers learning. Yet the main deliverable of most meetings is a binder full of *PowerPoint* slide printouts.

Assuming attendees don't leave their binders on the table at the end of the meeting ... where do they usually end up? On someone's shelf back in the office, never to be touched again until they are finally trashed when the employee moves.

It's no better to give out a CD containing all the presentations. This is just a cheaper way to produce something that's still useless. Have you ever actually loaded a meeting CD and fired up one of the presentations for review? No? Even if you did, how much sense did it make considering you didn't have the presenter's narration to go with it? Not much?

Too expensive.

The overall costs of such meetings are ridiculous. Most of the budget is devoted to logistics that deliver no added value: travel, food, housing, meeting room, meals, snacks, A/V directors, equipment, entertainment, and so on.

Plus, there are enormous indirect costs. In the earlier example, the productivity of the marketing department came to a screeching halt for six weeks before every annual meeting as the product managers focused on writing their slides, endlessly revising them, getting them approved, and rehearsing their presentations. And don't forget our story from Chapter 2.5 of $10 million in lost sales opportunity cost.

One and done.

Meetings are a single event that have no refresh learning process associated with them. You've seen the research. Long term, what do attendees have to show for the meeting? Nothing.

Too inefficient.

All this is for what? Having attendees say, "You know, I got two or three good ideas from that one-day meeting." Three good ideas max? In 480 minutes of presentations? One idea every two hours and 40 minutes? Are you serious? And management thinks this is a good idea?

There is a simple learning point to take away from this:

▨ *Enough already with the big meetings!*

Traditional big meetings are the ultimate lose-lose. The organization spends tons of money and yet has little to show for it. Why? Because the entire focus is on the content and not on the attendees. All that matters is what's being shown versus what's being learned.

▷ To Do
Somebody has to be an advocate for the attendees of big meetings, and that typically falls into Training's lap.
1. You need to start including the realities of attention span and cognitive load in your conversations with constituencies outside of Training. Everyone needs to understand the problems big meetings cause learners, and how ineffective these events are.
2. Although everyone moans about having to sit through meetings, management is not aware of the factors involved. Training needs to position itself as the SME on improving employee performance. Replacing big meetings with effective e-learning is a great way to do it.
3. Show this chapter to your meeting planners and executives.

Whew! We feel so much better now having gotten that off our chest. See you at next year's marketing meeting…

What's Wrong with Click-and-Read

THE CEO OF A REGIONAL HOSPITAL once told us that his holding company requires him to complete 17 hours of e-learning annually. The programs are the classic screen-flipping nightmares (i.e., totally useless). So he waits until Fall, buys a case of beer, and then spends an entire weekend watching football beside his laptop.

He discovered that the courses have a mandatory 7-second delay for each screen. So he sits there clicking on the Forward button about every 10 seconds while watching games. When the program won't advance any more, he knows he's reached a quiz. He completes it and then starts the next section.

A weekend of beer-soaked sports later, he has satisfied his annual training requirements. And we're sure the holding company's Training department is bragging to management about the comprehensive executive development program they provide.

Welcome to the world of click-and-read e-learning. This is defined as online training programs with these characteristics:

- Courses are 30 minutes to 3 hours in length.
- Courses consist of a series of discrete screens.
- Screens contain static graphics and text.
- On-screen text is narrated word for word.
- Course modules are separated by test sections.

Optionally, click-and-read courses may also contain the following:
- Animated graphics.

- A slide list indicating course position and slide time, with the ability to jump navigate to individual slides.
- A talking-head video window.

This approach is currently the most prevalent e-learning format available, with an enormous inventory of existing courses available off the shelf. Unfortunately, the typical implementation suffers from a number of problems that depress learning and limit its effectiveness. You've seen the relevant research. We can apply it here.

Topic versus task.

Like almost all kinds of training—classroom or e-learning—programs tend to be subject oriented rather than task focused. Courses teach topics versus skills, and learners are left to make the applicable link to their everyday tasks. This makes it harder for learners to generate business results.

Boring.

An endless string of static slides that are formally read to you is excruciatingly boring. Just ask our healthcare CEO watching TV. e-Learning expert Karl Kapp has observed:

> "The newer generation of workers is simply not going to tolerate these boring attempts at online learning."[1]

Here is a key question: Have you ever done your e-mail while participating in a webcast or taking an online course? Answer: Sure, we all have. They have simply been too boring to focus our entire attention on them.

Too long.

Nothing is more demoralizing that firing up a new e-learning program and seeing "Slide 1 of 124" in the navigation bar. It's the same old cognitive load and workplace interruption issue. There is too much information presented at one time, and employees can't block out that much contiguous time without interruptions.

Too inflexible.

Many click-and-read courses severely limit navigation options, forcing learners to sequentially click through every screen in a module before reaching the section test. This feature is one of the biggest student dissatisfaction points with e-learning.

Then why do it? Because it keeps learners from skipping directly to the test and bypassing the teaching content. Building in these kinds of restrictions is tacit acknowledgement by the instructional designer that the course is too long, too boring, and not compelling.

Limiting navigation options also has the effect of ruining the course for refresh learning or performance support. There is no way for students to quickly access a bit of content and then get back to work. They have to retake an applicable section in its entirety. And if they aren't sure where something is located, they may have to view multiple complete sections to find it. End result? They don't even try to find it.

Too formal.

Because text is fully written out, the language is usually formal in nature. Often it's written in a third-person voice where the language is like a term paper. This distances learners from the topic and lowers learning.

Word-for-word narration.

We've seen previously that word-for-word narration of on-screen text impedes learning. It fails to correctly utilize the audio loop in working memory, and it increases cognitive load in the visual sketchpad.

Incorrect use of visuals and text.

Many click-and-read programs seem designed to maximize split attention. In Chapter 4.5, you saw the rules for handling the various types of on-screen content, both individually and together. The typical click-and-read screen with detailed text, a decorative picture, and full-text narration violates those guidelines and depresses learning.

Inclusion of seductive content.
Those decorative pictures are seductive details. They are usually included mainly to dress up a plain text screen. There may also be other seductive content inserted to break up sections that instructional designers fear are too long. Either way, the research is clear. Seductive content reduces learning.

Grouped test questions.
As we've seen, research shows that you get the most mileage out of test questions by distributing them throughout a course rather than lumping them together at the end of sections. Practice exercises should be as close to the content being taught as possible.

Limited deployment options.
Click-and-read course development tools are designed primarily for deployment to a PC screen, which precludes delivery to most mobile devices. In addition, course developers depend on the large screen sizes to legibly display the detailed graphics and small fonts used in the slides. This makes handheld device deployment of that content impossible.

These problems are mostly due to the inherent limitations of the click-and-read format for e-learning. But they are also partly the problem of historical design practices typically used in click-and-read programs. Regardless, the result is inconvenience for the learner, low student engagement, and less retention of the content—which leads to uncertain business results. This is just not an effective way to train employees.

▷ To Do

You need to understand how much your current online courses violate the research on adult learning.

1. Examine your current stable of online programs. Start with those you have acquired from third-party vendors. The vast majority of these will probably be classic click-and-read legacy courses. Vendors have not yet updated their massive existing course

inventories for digital media and mobile deployment because it is too expensive to completely redevelop their entire product line.

2. Do the same for your online courses developed in-house. Many Training departments have chosen the click-and-read format for their own benefit—because it's a quick way to convert classroom training and the development tools are inexpensive—and not because this benefits learners.[2]

3. Look at your usage statistics. Training likes to tell management about how many online courses are available. Yet usage logs may show that nobody is completing them unless they are mandatory. Employees vote with their eyeballs, and their usage will tell you if your training is compelling.

Click-and-read is the most prevalent form of e-learning in use today, primarily because of its convenience in developing content. Clearly, research shows that it is not the best way to provide distance learning.

5.4

Issues with Webinars
(Live Click-and-Read)

A SPECIAL CLASS OF THE CLICK-AND-READ learning experience is the online webinar, which seems to present a number of advantages to organizations:

- Webinars are cheaper than holding meetings.
- Attendees just need to be at a PC.
- The only development required is a *PowerPoint* presentation.
- Attendees can interact live with the presenter.
- Anyone can access a recording of the webcast afterwards.

The two advantages mentioned most often are low cost and interaction. Webinar fees are only a few cents per minute per attendee, and the technology lets attendees communicate with presenters in real time through a conference phone call, a chat window, and click interactions. This is an attractive combination for Training departments, which have driven the widespread adoption of webinars across organizations of all sizes.

Once again, though, the focus of this solution is on the organization itself, not on learners. Management is operating on the assumption that webinars offer all the benefits of live instruction along with all the efficiencies of online communication. The reality is something different.

Learning analyst Elliott Masie wrote about one of the "dirty" secrets of the learning world—the high rate of no-shows for live virtual events such as webinars. Organizations report no-show rates as high as 40% to 60%.[1] Search the Internet for tips on effective webinars and you'll find that most of the articles start with a discussion of all the bad webcasts the authors have encountered. So what's going on?

Unattractive learning experience.

It starts with the basic premise of the webinar itself—that people want to watch static content while listening to a disembodied voice. It just isn't a great learning environment.

Imagine if a trainer told prospective students, "I hope you'll attend my upcoming class. I'm going to stand out of sight behind the projection screen and present a series of *PowerPoint* slides for 50 minutes. There will be 10 minutes of Q&A time provided at the end. If you have any questions before that, please write them down and give them to my assistant who will pass the notes on to me. I'll answer them if I have time. If there aren't too many attendees, I may open things up for a live discussion. Oh, and I also might give you some multiple choice questions to answer."

How eager would you be to attend this class? Not excited? Who would be?

Unique presenter skills required.

For many trainers, webinars are well outside their comfort zone and skill set. Many of the classroom presentation skills that make trainers successful don't work in webinars because there is no face-to-face communication and no attendee feedback.

In fact, the skill set that is the most helpful for webcasting is broadcasting. Radio hosts are used to talking to an invisible distant audience, interacting with co-hosts, keeping the topic moving, speaking clearly, staying vocally energized, dealing with callers over the phone, and handling a lot of production inputs at once.

Getting the worst and missing the best.

Webinars inherit many of the worst elements of click-and-read e-learning, and they omit the best element of classroom training. Webinars are often long, boring, visually unexciting, impersonal narrations of some SME's slide deck, just like a click-and-read course.

Then both the presenter and the attendees miss out on true personal interaction. Attendees can't watch for verbal cues as the trainer presents, and the trainer can't observe attendees' reactions to the content. At best, the trainer might have a real-time matrix of colored dots indicating how satisfied attendees are with the webinar, but that's about it for feedback.

Real-time limitations.

The real-time nature of webinars creates an either-or convenience versus interaction dilemma. If attendees want the opportunity to ask questions, then they have to be in front of their PC at a certain time. By definition, this makes webinars standard anticipation learning with all the issues that entails.

A learner can certainly view a recording of the program after the webinar. But this eliminates the opportunity for interaction with the presenter, which is one of the primary reasons to do a webcast in the first place. For post-viewers, the webinar essentially becomes a standard e-learning course. In that case, why not create a real e-learning program with the right instructional design to begin with?

Interruption friendly.

Have you ever checked your e-mail during a webcast? Sure, we all have. Webinars face a difficult attendee environment where it's easy to be interrupted or to focus attention on something else. In a webinar, learners merely need to stay logged in. They can be doing other work or talking to co-workers and nobody knows the difference.

Interactions, but no engagement.

Despite the capability for interaction, communication is often one-way from the presenter to attendees. This can happen due to a variety of reasons. There may be too much content for the time allowed, so there's no opportunity for questions. The presenter may not be able to deal with questions coming in and continue teaching at the same time. The presenter may not be comfortable with the technology.

As a result, the live communication capability is often little used And when it is utilized, it may be more to confirm attendees' involvement (i.e., making them do something that tells the presenter they're still there and awake), rather than to provide practice or to test learning.

No scorecard move-the-needle measures.
For many organizations, attending the webinar is itself the completion event. Students are assumed to have learned from having been logged in throughout the entire session.

In terms of business results, there is little research addressing how webinars compare with other learning events. Most discussions of webcast effectiveness point out their value in generating sales leads.

Now all those no-shows begin to make sense. Webinars present trainers with a learning environment that looks simple on the surface—just give your *PowerPoint* presentation over the Web instead of in front of an audience. Yet the skills required are quite unique and sophisticated. Still, even when everything is done right, the learning environment is not one that students would prefer if given the choice.

◑ To Do
Conducting a successful webinar is not much different than delivering a live classroom seminar where presentation equipment is involved. Trainers need to work to get the most out of a difficult learning situation.

1. As always, any training event starts with compelling content. That can help make up for the limitations of the webinar experience.
2. Minimize the Terrible Too's by complying with the e-learning instructional design rules in Part 4. You can't ignore them just because this is a live event.
3. Slides for a webinar are different than slides for a presentation. You may need more or less slide detail for a webinar, depending on the topic. It all depends on the pace of the presentation and how long each slide will be on-screen. You want to engage your attendees' eyes without overloading their visual sketchpad.

4. You need to develop your webinar presentation skills. This means focusing specifically on your vocal skills for speaking clarity, pace, inflection, range, and so on. For example, there are certain vocal traits that make you more credible or more persuasive.[2]

   You should record yourself and compare your vocal performance to broadcast radio hosts. They are who your attendees listen to and are comparing you with.

5. You need to develop standards for your webinars. It isn't a simple task.

Webinars are not going away. They are a cheap way to provide live training without having to gather everyone in one place, but they're all too often perfect examples of the Terrible Too's of training.

The Dangers of Social Media

A FEW YEARS BACK we were taking a graduate business program in one of those accelerated evening formats, meeting one night per week for eight weeks. The instructor was not particularly industrious, and after a half-hearted lecture the first night he broke us into six teams. Each one was assigned to provide one week's lecture. The last session of the term consisted of a review and the final exam, with grades being based only on the presentations and the final. So for the rest of the term, the instructor's role was to just sit there.

One of our team members, a very funny guy, was livid. He said, "Look, nothing against you all, it's about me, too. I enrolled in this program because there were supposed to be educators who are also leading business practitioners. I didn't enroll to learn from a bunch of people who are as stupid as I am." He went on to call it the "idiots teaching idiots" approach, and we all had a good laugh about it.

We finished the course and got our grades, although it certainly wasn't the best course we'd ever taken. But that phrase stuck with us, particularly with all the current interest in the latest hot training topic, "social learning."

From an academic viewpoint, social learning is a teaching method where students learn through talking among themselves.[1] Each participant is responsible for learning what is taught and for helping others to learn. An instructor (i.e., a leader who knows the assignment and the solution) may not be involved. In fact, the instructor, when present, may not even have an idea as to the ultimate problem and solution participants will end up working on.

You can argue that social learning is essentially what employees do every day. Experienced co-workers answer questions from novices. Managers coach subordinates. Work teams address departmental issues. Process teams pool their shared experience to solve specific defects. Vendors and customers share best practices within their supply chains.

Social media software takes this to a new level. It provides the capability for an unlimited number of people to collaborate. Experts can distribute information in blogs. Employees can post questions to topical chat sites. Customers can share experiences on product pages. The benefits seem extensive. Social learning can:

- Leverage the collective knowledge of the organization and its constituents.
- Connect participants who have similar issues and interests.
- Increase participant involvement and satisfaction.
- Break down barriers and silos.
- Increase teamwork.
- Speed up communication.
- Share best practices for ideas and solutions.
- Reduce costs versus classroom training and e-learning.

This all sounds wonderful. So is social learning a great way to develop workers, or is it idiots teaching idiots? With organizations so eager to adopt social learning systems, it's important to understand the issues they create.

Questionable sources.

A hidden and basically unchallenged assumption of social learning is that a group of interested people can solve any problem. What no one talks about is whether or not those people are *qualified* to solve that problem. To be qualified, they must not only possess the right knowledge and skills but also have *perspective* concerning the issue. They need to understand the bigger issues of how any potential solutions will affect the organization overall.

If you're not careful, social media systems become incredibly efficient ways to quickly disseminate incorrect information. For example, you wouldn't want a group of your neighbors to check with each other on a social media site and then operate on your brain. You want one skilled neurosurgeon for the job. Yet social learning suggests that the team approach is the way to go. Or better yet, that you post a question to a healthcare social media site and get advice from a bunch of strangers on how you can do it yourself.

Data fragmentation and risk.

We saw a presentation that identified nearly 60 different social media sites, and this was only a partial list. The comment was that this large number of social media tools can be overwhelming for organizational users. The presentation went on to note that proprietary institutional knowledge can end up scattered all over the Internet, with the corresponding concerns about data privacy and security.[2]

The result is that institutional knowledge can end up fragmented across different systems. Even with a single in-house system, data quickly become separated by topic and interest group. This makes it difficult to stay abreast of the ever-changing content regardless of where the data reside. It also makes it difficult to identify and consolidate related information in different locations.

There is also a data redundancy issue. It's almost unavoidable that the same information will need to be entered into the various social learning systems, both for user identification and for the content itself. Have one thing change, and you'll likely need to post updates to multiple sites.

Lost productivity.

In addition to data security issues, social media creates massive productivity issues. A 2007 Basex study found that interruptions from online collaboration tools took up 28% of a knowledge worker's day and that the overall cost in lost productivity in the United States was an estimated $588 billion.[3]

The last thing most organizations want is for their employees to regularly visit even more social media sites—whether internal or external. What seems like a more efficient way to communicate can quickly become extreme time-wasting.

Legal exposure.

The strength of social media is that it involves everyone. The weakness of social media is that it involves everyone.

The very nature of an open communication forum creates legal and public relations risks. Abusive comments are formally under the organizational banner when they're posted on internal social media sites. These comments are now part of the official record, no matter how quickly they're removed.

There is also an embarrassment factor. Vendors have been surprised when buyers have posted product complaints on customer support websites. It becomes a no-win situation. Leave unfair or inaccurate comments online and let potential customers see them. Or remove the comments, and be accused of censoring in order to deceive future buyers.

Social media presents a high risk. All you have to do is visit a few online sites and check out the comments posted below the articles. You quickly see how many of the posters are absolute crackpots who have outlandish positions, who viciously attack other posters, or who go off topic because they have some other personal axe to grind and figure this is a captive audience. Social learning gives all of these nuts a public forum on your website.

These reasons are why social media has been slow to catch on with employers. It's an everyday part of personal life, but it's filled with danger from an organizational standpoint.

▷ To Do

Social learning appears to offer significant value and cost advantages, but the practice is different than the promise.

1. Be ready to talk to your management about social media. The subject is going to come up whether you are ready or not.
2. Study the applicability of social learning in your organization. Create a pilot, if indicated, and then evaluate it on the basis of the factors mentioned previously. Prepare recommendations for the role, if any, that you see for social media in your organization.
3. Be proactive. Don't wait until you're asked about social media. Include the results of your study in your next training update with management.
4. If you're asked to implement a social learning system, insist that there be sufficient monitors assigned to each department, division, topic, product, etc., on the site or platform. Their job is to visit their site daily, read all comments, correct inaccuracies, provide help when needed, and remove violators. Monitors are the experts often missing in the process.

The topic of social media links directly with Chapter 1.3, "Treat Training as a Profession." Certainly, peers can help each other by sharing expertise and helping with problems. But training is a formal process that requires specialized knowledge and skills. You need to make certain that management understands the serious ramifications of converting formal training delivered by professionals into informal and unvalidated learning delivered by peers.

Games, Simulations, and Virtual Worlds

OK, BEFORE YOU EVEN REALIZE WHAT HAS HAPPENED, you're sitting in front of the TV with a game controller in hand, talking strategy with the eight-year-old at your side. The topic of discussion is what you both need to do immediately as a group of storm troopers come around the corner and begin shooting at you.

What makes this so surreal, and your adult involvement so ridiculous, is that your Jedi knight is a block character in an all-Lego Star Wars universe. And yet you are *hooked.* Your palms are sweating. You are totally concentrating. You are *there.* As a result, you end up spending all day in what is essentially an 8-hour interactive commercial for Legos.

Don't feel bad. You're not alone. Here are some surprising market data from the Entertainment Software Association:

- 72% of American households play computer or video games.
- 58% of game players are male.
- The average age of a game player is 37.
- More older adults than children play games. 29% of game players are 50 and older in age, and only 18% are 17 and younger.
- More adult women than juvenile males play games. 37% of game players are women age 18 and older, and only 13% are boys younger than 17.[1]

It's clear that playing games is an adult activity, and not just for males. The result is a $25 billion annual industry in the United States and a $56 billion business worldwide with an expected growth to $82 billion by 2015.[2]

It's only natural that organizations see the power of video games to capture peoples' attention and wonder how that could be leveraged for worker development. Standard industry game categories already include job-related genres such as strategy, simulation, skill (driving, flight, etc.), and role-playing. It seems to be just a matter of applying these concepts to workplace learning and figuring out where game concepts can benefit an organization. Here are some factors to consider.

Simulations.

The premise of simulation-based training is that, as the workplace continues to become more complex, employees need more than skill and knowledge competencies. They also need the ability to adapt to changing circumstances. They could potentially get that on the job, but this experience can be costly and time-consuming to obtain depending upon how big a problem mistakes cause.

Simulations can be used to create environments that mimic the real-world workplace, where assignments can be dealt with in context. Simulations can also provide realistic practice environments for tasks that are dangerous or that occur infrequently such as disaster management. Or they can provide artificial environments that are impossible in the real world.[3] Need to put someone on the surface of the sun? In an engine cylinder? On a growing plant? A simulation can do it, yet there are major issues.

The first concern is that of training effectiveness. Although a number of anecdotal successes have been reported, multiple research studies have failed to find an advantage for simulation-based training. Most studies have examined simulations in K-12 classrooms. Additional research is necessary for understanding the effects on training adults on business skills.[4]

The second concern is that there are no established design standards for simulations like there are for traditional training. This is partly due to the fact that it is hard to compare the two. Simulation learning teaches implicit and contextual knowledge, which traditional measures such as tests cannot document. So it's difficult to definitively prove A is better than B.

The third concern is employee acceptance. The assumption is that learners prefer simulation learning because it is more fun than traditional classroom or e-learning. Yet many employees feel more comfortable with a straightforward teaching format, especially for critical functions.[5] Rather than learning by discovery, they are saying, "Tell me what to do."

The fourth concern with simulations is the cost. Each hour of simulation is estimated to require between 750 and 1,500 hours of development.[6] Also, it's important to understand that a one-hour simulation doesn't mean that only an hour of content has to be developed. Total possible course time can be much higher than the student course time, depending upon the number and complexity of the alternate paths provided. It's just that no one student will see all of it in any single pass through the simulation.

The final concern is the classic one of seductive content. Traditional training is certainly better for straight information and process content. The unique factors simulation-based training offers are rich content, immersion, interactivity, communication, and learner control—all in real time. This can be quite powerful, but it also provides opportunities for cognitive overload and inefficiencies. Simulations can be crowd-pleasing but inefficient ways to convey learning points. If a picture or story can depress learning, just imagine what a game can do. The mental load of operating the simulation can easily override the embedded skills being taught.

Virtual worlds.

The latest variation in simulation training is virtual worlds. An outgrowth of role-playing games, virtual worlds allow workers to exist in a three-dimensional (3D) simulated setting. Here learners create an avatar of themselves that can communicate with others and that can originate and use objects.

This is a very engaging environment. Learners are immersed in their world as an independent person. That world can be highly realistic, from advanced graphics to photo-accurate. The user has freedom of movement and communication to "live" in this world, as well as interact with it and other visitors.

Although this approach is costly from a training standpoint, it can be less expensive than real life. But there's a heavy overhead price to pay for creating and maintaining a 3D world, whether developed internally or hosted elsewhere. And there are built-in inefficiencies in having students experience the world versus learning through a curriculum. There is also the key question as to how much of the virtual world experience is seductive content versus specific learning.

It's all about the justification. Simulation learning might be useful when:
- The payback from training is great.
- Training is for implicit "apply" knowledge.
- Traditional training methods have not proven effective.
- Managers are unable to coach the required skills on the job.
- On-the-job learning curve mistakes cannot be tolerated.
- Content is structured enough to minimize seductive content elements and inefficiencies from student-driven interaction with the simulation.
- There is a sufficient enough student population to spread the development cost.
- Content is relatively stable and does not require constant reprogramming.

Note that simulation is an option when other approaches have not proven effective and when there is sufficient justification for the additional effort and cost. Although there are discussions on the benefits of simulation training, to date we've seen limited data on the *payback* for simulations over other methods.

◯ To Do
You need to be prepared to discuss this whole area of game-inspired training.

1. If you haven't already, familiarize yourself with the capabilities of game-like simulation sites and services. As you do, pay careful attention to how efficient this approach is, and what learner skills are required to utilize it.
2. Think about whether or not this approach could be useful in your organization, and what costs would be involved. Ask yourself if Training wants to get involved in a full IT level project such as creating and maintaining a virtual world and if it makes sense for the organization.
3. Be ready to discuss this approach with management should they ask. Along with social media, this is one of those hot topics that management is seeing in the business press.

In general, simulation learning is a niche tool for very specialized training applications. Its overall effectiveness versus traditional training methods is still in question, there is a major learning curve, and the cost requirements are significant.

Mobile When and How

TALK ABOUT A TOUGH INDUSTRY TO BE IN. How would you like to run a pay phone company? It's a dying business that is being played out to the end by small regional companies since the major carriers abandoned it. The mobile phone revolution started the decline, and the 2009 federal Lifeline program giving free cellphones and minutes to people on welfare was the final blow.[1] Imagine if you were a pay phone company and were not adjusting accordingly. Well, that's exactly what many organizations are doing with the mobile revolution.

Another one of those questions that generate a blank look from trainers is, "What is your mobile learning strategy?"

As this is written, mobile deployment of training is in the early adopter phase. According to the American Society for Training & Development, only about one in five organizations uses some kind of mobile employee training, and those applications tend to be limited in scope.[2,3] Contrast this with Google, which in 2010 announced its "mobile first" decision to create new applications for smartphones before creating ones to run on PCs.[4]

The concept of mobile learning has a lot going for it. Mobile devices are now fully capable computers in their own right. Their screens offer high-quality displays. They are advanced multimedia devices with a variety of data input options.

This allows organizations to deliver sophisticated mobile learning programs that fit the requirements for effective adult learning. Content can be given in small bites. Training can minimize anticipation learning by delivering just-in-time content directly at the point of use. And the always-with-you nature of smartphones—versus the sometimes-with-you nature of tablets or PCs—enables performance support applications where a handheld mobile device becomes the go-to source for process help and up-to-the-minute information.

The big reason for the slow adoption rate is that mobile learning more than doubles the work load and costs for Training departments. This is because organizations are using a "create many, deploy once" approach in which there are different versions of programs for various devices.

The first problem is that much of the e-learning being developed today is unsuitable for mobile deployment. Click-and-read or converted *PowerPoint* programs are single-deployment designs requiring larger screen sizes. Websites are designed to be accessed by PCs. Video is shot to be viewed on a standard-sized screen.

With all of them, program elements become unreadable when seen on a handheld device screen because of small font sizes, fine detail on graphics, and long-shot video framing. Certainly, zooming and scrolling is possible, but it is unwieldy and bothersome. It's like watching a football game through a toilet paper roll, and users won't put up with it. Mobile deployment means creating whole new versions of existing and future programs.

The second problem is one of device incompatibility. In the PC world, organizations issue systems to employees. It's easy to maintain hardware and software standards that simplify deployment. In the mobile arena, employees bring their own devices to the organization, so there's a variety of hardware and software being used. Mobile applications have to run on *all* of them. This is further complicated by the fact that, even with individual vendors, mobile devices are rapidly changing in terms of operating systems, software release versions, and hardware.

The result is a dramatic increase in costs to go mobile and support all your workers' devices. This is true *unless you create content* now *that runs on any mobile platform without redevelopment.*

With all this in mind, here are recommendations for adding mobile programs to your training capabilities.

Develop backwards from the small screen.

You need to stop developing programs that only run on a large screen. That's a dead-end approach that will be ever more obsolete as mobile devices become the platform of choice for workers. To minimize the costs of duplicate development, what you want is a "create once, deploy many" design that runs relatively unchanged regardless of the device. This means you must chunk up information into smaller bites, use large fonts, segment and simplify graphics to show all the details, shoot video with a tighter frame, and specify to the lowest common denominator of mobile device features.

Keep it *really* short.

We've talked about a typical adult attention span of 5 to 15 minutes. When it comes to mobile viewing, attention span is even shorter. Programs need to be in the 1- to 3-minute range. You should be thinking more "TV commercial" than "training program."

Minimize content.

You now know all about cognitive load. Think of the mobile environment as requiring mini-cognitive load. Mobile content needs to be just enough to complete a task and get back to work.

One way to minimize content is to prioritize and edit down. Not everything on a website is critical, and not everything in a training program is a "must-do."

Another way to minimize content is to chunk it up. One program may become multiple programs. One site may be broken up into several related sites for mobile users. Multi-column pages can become separate single-column pages, with no more than two screens of scrolling down needed for any one page.

Simplify navigation.

The typical menu bar of options doesn't fit across the top of a mobile screen. Plus, putting all the required navigation on a single-column page can push the actual content down off the mobile screen.

Consider segmenting the navigation. Some mobile sites put navigation at the bottom of a screen where users can scroll to it if they need it. Or the main navigation and site search is on the Home page, and content is placed on separate screens. Navigation might even be a drop-down menu.

Recognize the capability for input.

Depending upon the model, mobile devices have a number of input options including text, voice, pictures, and video (front and rear facing). Unlike PC users, who are often limited to keyboard input only, mobile users can be effective multimedia content *creators.* This means that the one way push-to-users model of training can be expanded to a push-pull bi-directional model. Institutional knowledge residing outside of Training can now be more easily captured and leveraged.

Accommodate touchscreen and non-touchscreen users.

You can't always be certain that users have touchscreen smartphones. Some phones still in use only have trackballs, joysticks, or direction keys. Remember, you need to design for the lowest common denominator.

Also, factor in the practical issues of using a touchscreen. What looks good on a PC can be impossible to use on a mobile device. We've all mistakenly called the wrong person due to accidently selecting an adjacent link. Big fingers touching a tiny screen can make it very difficult to tap on small buttons or links, especially if several are in close proximity onscreen.

There are many other design recommendations we could include, but these highlight the main structural differences between PC-oriented applications and those developed for mobile deployment.

○ To Do
Accept the fact that mobile learning is in your future. So it's very simple:
1. You need to have a mobile learning element in your training plan.
2. Decide when and where there's the most potential benefit for a mobile solution.
3. Get your feet wet. Start a small trial of the technology and get going up the learning curve. You want to have this process figured out *before* management assigns you to do it.
4. Where you have a solid business case, justify the time and budget and then implement your pilot mobile training application. There will certainly be more to come as the training industry shifts from classroom and PC-based anticipation learning to on-the-job, just-in-time training and performance support.

It's not a question of "Should we do mobile?" The question is, "When and how do we best do mobile?" It's going to happen, because it is a must-do from the user's perspective. The challenge is how to add mobile programs to your mix without tripling or quadrupling your development costs for training. That's the topic of our next chapter.

Why Short-Form Video

OK, THE RESEARCH SO FAR has not been very positive about any of the common methods of training. So what's left? Video!

Video isn't exactly the new kid when it comes to learning technology. It has been used in one form or another by educators since the early days of film, and its effects have been formally studied for over 70 years. Yet the use of video content for workplace training has historically been fairly limited, consisting mostly of showing third-party training videos or clips from movies during seminars.

We didn't start out as video enthusiasts. If anything, we've had the most traditional of classroom and CBT experiences. But throughout our careers, we've always been medium agnostic. The best technology to use was whatever research showed would move the needle the most.

Today, research points strongly to online video as the best way to generate business results and create a quick payback for training projects. We're not alone in our enthusiasm for video. Comments like these are common.

From the *New York Times*: "Sometimes—and this is a difficult sentence for a newspaper to print—it's easier to learn from a video."[1]

From the Center for Public Broadcasting: "According to educator surveys and research, educational television:
• Reinforces reading and lecture material.
• Aids in the development of a common base of knowledge among students.

- Enhances student comprehension and discussion.
- Provides greater accommodation of diverse learning styles.
- Increases student motivation and enthusiasm."[2]

From Forrester Research: "Video greatly enhances the message quality and experience ... Content delivered with video has a much higher retention rate."[3]

From the *American Journal of Distance Education:* "There was a significant difference in learners' motivation in terms of attention between video-based instruction and traditional text-based instruction. In addition, learners reported that the video-based instruction was more memorable than the traditional text-based instruction."[4]

From Cisco CEO John Chambers: "If you think about the innovation that occurred in the '90s, that was about transforming business models ... your ability to communicate with others through e-mail first, then text and now video. Video will be the killer app in the Internet. And it will obviously be in different forms of unified communications."[5]

From training guru Elliott Masie: "The introduction of video into almost every aspect of our learning and work tasks is profound ... 2011 is the year of video."[6,7]

Digital video is riding a perfect storm of user preference, bandwidth growth, mobile device capabilities, and entry-level production technology. Video also provides the best match with the research on adult learning:

Most comfortable medium.

We're all professional TV watchers. According to Neilsen, the average American views over 151 hours of TV per month.[8] Does any of this video take the form of click-and-read e-learning or talking head plus static slides? Of course not. No one would watch anything that boring.

Everything from entertainment news to sports reviews is presented like the evening weather report with a presenter integrated with the content.

Benefit of an on-screen presenter.

Research shows that students learn more when there is an on-screen agent presenting the information.[9] The easiest way to do that is with a human presenter. Video gives learners the look and feel of the live event with an e-learning delivery.

Easy to create.

It used to be that video required a large studio, a massive investment in equipment, and media experts to produce it. Now grade schools are turning out their own internal shows in evening news TV format. Digital video equipment and computer technology have dramatically dropped in price. Even consumer devices now include a video camera or two as standard equipment, and there are various options to add lenses, microphones, and mounts. As a result, the challenge for training has shifted from how to do video to how to do it right.

Manages cognitive load. (Chapter 3.1 and 3.2)

Video takes advantage of the visual sketchpad and audio loop capabilities of working memory. Properly designed programs minimize overloading either subsystem and provide a familiar and controlled way for students to learn content.

Matches short attention span needs. (Chapter 3.3)

Video is an ideal short-form medium. Programs can easily be kept within the 5- to 15-minute attention-span window and assembled in a series to address bigger topics.

Non-linear access for refresh learning. (Chapter 3.4)

One of the problems with the use of videotape in training was its linear nature. It often took longer to cue up a clip you wanted to show than it did to show the segment itself.

The beauty of digital video is that it can be accessed non-linearly. You can immediately jump to specific sections or drag a slider bar along to find the specific frame you want to view. This opens up digital video to a whole new range of uses such as refresh learning and performance support.

Minimizes anticipation learning. (Chapter 3.5)
If it is shot properly for the small screen (and that is a big "if" for many organizations), video can be delivered at a moment's notice to anywhere a learner is working. This reduces the anticipation learning delay to zero.

Eliminates split attention. (Chapter 4.5)
By integrating the presenter with the content—à la the evening news weather report—learners are looking at only a single window of information. And, as discussed previously, on-screen presenters can focus attention on themselves or their content through the proper presentation techniques.

Engagement provides necessary interaction. (Chapter 4.6)
In the past, trainers have been reluctant to use video because it was seen as a passive medium generating low involvement from learners. You now know that this is not necessarily the case. Video programs created with properly designed elements of engagement provide the same or better results than e-learning with physical click interactions.

Deployable to all six screens. (Chapter 5.7)
As we highlighted in the previous chapter, content today must be delivered to all "six screens" (smartphones, tablets, PCs, portable media players, route handhelds, and TVs). Video is the *only* medium that can be deployed to all these without redevelopment. This provides an enormous cost and time savings to organizations, while actually *improving* training results.

Can be used as is for five different purposes. (Chapter 6.6)
We will talk about this in a coming chapter, but video turns a "create many, deploy once" training architecture into a more cost-effective "create once, deploy many" approach. This is another contributor to the major cost advantage video provides trainers.

Can be redeployed internationally.
Video provides a standardized way to quickly deploy content in multiple languages. For a full conversion, an original program can be converted in a series of standard steps: transcribe the program, translate the script and slides, have a local language SME edit them, and then have a local language presenter record the program from a teleprompter. For a quick conversion, all you need to do is make the video closed-captioned in the local language. (Some organizations even prefer this approach because it helps viewers improve their English skills.)

All this is why many organizations are now using online digital video as their primary (and in some cases their only) vehicle for training and communication. It's a perfect fit for the requirements of today's workplace, it meets the standards for effective adult learning, and it is cost-effective in doing this.

▷ To Do
Similar to mobile deployment in the previous chapter, it's not a matter of, "Are you going to get into video?" It's a matter of *when* you're going to adopt video as a major medium.

1. Accept the inevitable. The days of talking heads and static slides are long gone. If it doesn't look like TV, then it's not going to hold the attention of your learners.
2. Look at your off-the-shelf inventory of traditional e-learning programs, both internally and from vendors. Is anyone completing them by choice rather than by mandate? You need for that content to be not only compelling but also delivered in an engaging fashion.

3. Review your development plans. How many coming programs are dead ends when it comes to mobile deployment? Start analyzing how much it's going to save your organization to start doing as much as you can in a medium that can be deployed everywhere. Otherwise, in the future you'll be spending two or three times more than you should for multiple versions of the same programs.
4. Build a video content component into your training plan, and demand it from your vendors.

The use of digital video in learning is one of those rare situations where you can lower costs and actually *increase* results. This is why video e-learning and communication is not a "nice-to-do." It's a must-do.

Strategies to Support Training

SO FAR WE'VE FOCUSED primarily on how to make training itself more effective. That's only part of the performance improvement process. Learners need to actually apply new skills to the job at hand and move the needle.

To make this happen, trainers must extend their involvement outside the boundaries of the traditional training function in order to make certain their efforts are generating measurable payback in results. This means answering strategic questions such as:

How important are the factors surrounding training to its overall success?

What role does the manager play in training?

How can training be integrated into career development?

How can a Training department significantly reduce costs while maintaining effectiveness?

What is the process to test new training solutions?

Dividing Learning into Learn/Apply

HERE'S A FUNDAMENTAL ISSUE for you as a trainer. Can people learn to be great hitters by taking batting practice under the watchful eye of the batting coach? Can they become great golfers by taking lessons and then hitting buckets of balls at the range? In other words, is it possible to master a skill just by practicing it?

Most coaches will say that practice is essential in any sport, but that the only way to be great is to actually *play* the sport. No amount of practice in the batting cage or on the driving range can prepare you for real competition.

You can see the analogy. Trainers are focused on building workplace skills that move the needle on business results. You identify the proper content, organize it with an appropriate instructional design, and insert plenty of practice into the learning event. You've been doing this for years, yet the people at the big table still are not committing their checkbook to fully support training. According to research, what's missing? It's the live application part of the skills equation.

What we are talking about is "transfer of learning," which is when learners transfer new knowledge and skills into improved job performance. In most organizations, this transfer has not been successful.

- As mentioned in Chapter 1.1, in his 2000 book, *Transfer of Learning*, Robert Haskell stated: "Most of the research on employee training clearly shows that, although millions of dollars are spent on training in the public sector, there is little empirical evidence linking training to improved job behavior or employee attitudes."[1]

- In a 2007 *HRD Review* paper, Kay Bunch of Georgia State University begins, "Organizations spend as much as US$200 billion annually on training and development; however, much of this investment appears squandered on ill-conceived or poorly implemented interventions." The paper quotes numerous sources for evidence of training failure and goes on to evaluate how organizational culture contributes to it.[2]
- In a 2008 survey of a large number of employees who had just gone through training, 15% said they did not try the new skills on the job. 70% said they tried them and failed. Only 15% were able to successfully sustain the new behaviors.[3]

What's going on is that a learning event by itself cannot ensure mastery. You can supply the acquisition learning and the opportunity to practice, but you can't guarantee the transfer of learning. Here is research showing the importance of what happens *outside* of training.

- A 2004 University of Phoenix study found that 26% of learning effectiveness occurs before the learning event, and that 50% of learning effectiveness comes afterwards.[4]
- A 2008 Bersin & Associates study indicated that approximately 80% of all corporate learning takes place through on-the-job interactions with peers, experts, and managers.[5]
- A 2006 ASTD study on the causes of poor results from training found that 20% was due to events prior to training and 70% was due to problems in the "application environment." Only 10% of problems were related to the training itself.[6]

The ASTD study also found that problems with the transfer of learning after training were the result of two factors: (1) learners not having the opportunity to use the new knowledge and skills and (2) managers not reinforcing the new behaviors after the training event.[7]

What we're talking about is the difference between "learn" and "apply." It's clear that you cannot equate training participation with actual performance improvement. For example, it's good to practice a conflict management process in a pretend situation with other seminar attendees, but those skills are not going to be truly transferred until learners successfully use them with a customer yelling at them. And the skills won't be locked in until a manager praises learners for it afterwards.

Unfortunately, although the application side of learning is critical, this isn't where organizations are allocating their funds:

85% of training dollars are spent on the learning event itself. 10% of funds are spent on pre-work, and only 5% of funds are spent on follow-up to the training—which is where the big payoff is.[8]

It's the exact opposite of the 80-20 Rule. According to all this research, the vast majority of funds are being spent on the *least* valuable contributor to results.

Going back to the Bunch research, organizations are in need of a major cultural change regarding training. It starts with how the Training department views itself:

- Is it a function—to develop employees?
- Is it a tactic—to improve employee performance?
- Is it a manufacturer—to produce training events?
- Is it financial—to create one-year payback on the training investment?
- Is it strategic—to create a competitive advantage in time-to-market of knowledge and skills?

Ideally, training needs to fulfill all of these missions. But if your involvement is only training events, then you're just a manufacturer. Those other more important missions aren't possible.

The lesson is clear. Worker development cannot be the sole responsibility of the Training department. Learning isn't done in isolation.

◔ To Do

How do you get beyond the traditional view of the Training department?

1. Share this research with your Training department. It can be an important wake-up call.

2. See how your department compares with the research numbers. Are you in that 20-80 position regarding where you put your resources? Or are you ahead of the game with substantial "apply" practices in place?

3. Redefine your role, both internally and with management. You are not solely a manufacturer and deliverer of courses. You're the learning expert who can help integrate employee development throughout the organization.

4. Understand that, as a result of research here and in Part 3, you may need to dramatically reengineer your training processes. After seeing this, trainers often have the reaction, "Oh my, we're nowhere near where we need to be. It's no wonder we're fighting the problems we are."

5. Stay with it. Coming chapters will show you how to convert from a traditional training model to a learn/apply model focused on the successful transfer of learning.

An old African proverb is, "It takes a village to raise a child." For trainers, it requires an organization to educate an employee. That means expanding the reach of Training outside the traditional boundaries of stand-alone learning events.

It's Not a Program, It's a Process

ONE OF THE THINGS WE LIKED TO DO at the start of an AIM consulting engagement with consumer goods vendors was to ride with one of their top route salespeople.[1] We always made the point that we weren't there to evaluate anyone but rather to see the market area.

But no matter what we said, all the salespeople knew was that some strange dude from headquarters was spending the day with them, so they weren't taking any chances. They did everything by the book, exactly as they'd been taught to do.

We started one ride-along at about 7:00 a.m. and were scheduled to visit 21 accounts that day. At each stop, the salesperson was careful to do every step in the specified sales process. He walked the perimeter of the store looking for cross-merchandising opportunities. He faced products with labels forward in gravity shelves. He repackaged torn goods. He left the back room spotless.

By noon we had hit only seven of his accounts, and it was clear the poor guy was never going to get done unless we left him alone. There just weren't enough hours in the day. So we had him drop us off at the warehouse and let him get back to his route. We happened to see him later in the day at about 3:30 p.m. He had finished the other 14 accounts in 3½ hours. He was clearly skipping more than a few steps after we left.

In the previous chapter, we talked about the importance of all the things that go on before and after training. So what are the activities that have to surround training to make it successful? In *Building Expertise,*

Ruth Colvin Clark talks about creating a "culture of transfer" in organizations.[2] This culture makes certain that:

- Learners are given the opportunity to use new skills soon after training.
- They are allowed time to try new skills.
- Managers are able to coach on training content.
- Learners are rewarded for applying new skills.
- Learners are provided with sufficient pre- and post-training assistance for skills mastery.

This assures that learners will return to a work environment that supports the application of the new skills they have learned. It's the embodiment of a learn/apply model for employee development. Figure 6.2.1 shows this overall training process.

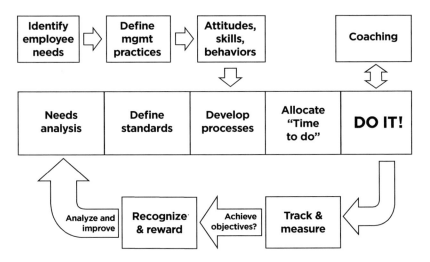

Figure 6.2.1: The Training Process.

It starts with a training research phase, which includes needs analysis, defining standards, and developing processes. These steps establish the "what" of training (i.e., the content to be taught). Organizations typically know what these are. This isn't a struggle for them.

The training phase is next. It includes identifying employee needs, defining management practices, and teaching the related attitudes, skills, and behaviors. This is the "how" of training (i.e., the classic functions of a Training department). Again, this is something most organizations can do, although as we've seen, the training may not be as efficient as it should be.

The time-to-do phase is often where things begin to break down, as they did in our ride-along with the salesperson. Employees must be allowed enough time to perform new processes to standards. This includes being given enough additional trial-and-error time during the learning curve period right after training. It also includes being given enough time to perform new procedures on a permanent basis once the new skills are mastered.

Training without sufficient time-to-do is a total waste of training resources. Unfortunately, what tends to happen is that duties are frequently added to processes, but there is no additional time built into the day to accomplish them.

That's exactly what had happened in our route example. Time-consuming steps such as walking the store were added to the sales process, but the number of daily stops stayed at 21. Something had to give. Orders were due in by 3:30 p.m., so that afternoon the salesperson simply wrote replenishment orders for his remaining accounts and skipped everything else.

The next phase is using the new skills on the job, which is another common source of breakdown. As you saw in the previous chapter, only 15% of employees in one study were able to "Do it!" successfully on a permanent basis. The reasons have a lot to do with the final two phases of the training process.

The Coaching phase is another frequent area of breakdown. Managers must support the training process. They need to coach new skills and reinforce the associated new behaviors. Without manager support, the low 15% success rate may be unavoidable. This is so critical that we're going to spend an upcoming chapter talking about it.

The final phase closes the loop on performance and is another common source for breakdown in the training process. The old saying applies here, "If you don't measure it, you can't manage it." The only way 85% of employees can fail to do what they've been trained to do is if no one cares about their performance. That could mean several things:

- No one is monitoring performance of the new skills.
- Performance is being tracked, but no one pays attention to the results.
- Results are being monitored, but nothing happens, good or bad.
- There are rewards and recognition, but no information is being used to improve the process.

When there's a breakdown in any of the steps within this feedback loop phase, then the message to learners is clear. "If the training is useful to you personally, good for you. Otherwise, nobody else here really cares if you use it or not. Just get your work done."

In our route situation, the message from management in effect was, "Here are all the things you're supposed to do to maximize both our sales and your commissions. But we're not going to give you enough time to do them all, and no one is going to monitor you to see if they're getting done. So do whatever you want. Just make sure you make your numbers. Live long and prosper."

Now you begin to see the reasons for the low training success rates quoted in the previous chapter. As a Training department, you may be doing everything right, yet the organization is seeing no results from your efforts. You create improved employees and then send them back to a work environment totally unprepared for their new skills. Or worse yet, you send them back to a situation where there is no hope of using their new skills. It's no wonder learners try to avoid training whenever they can.

◗ **To Do**

Everything from the previous chapter applies here. We're still talking about the need for a major cultural shift regarding training in organizations.

1. Expand your participation in personnel development projects. You need to be involved both earlier and later in the process.
2. Promote adequate time-to-do to implement new skills during the learning curve and for the new process on a continuing basis. It's better to halt the training project than to teach people how to do something that they have no time for.
3. Promote a functional feedback loop. If any track-and-measure breakdown conditions exist, you might once again be better off halting the training project.

We talked in Part 2 about the difficulty in establishing the value of training. Now you see that the lack of measurable payback can be due more to breakdowns in the training process than to problems with training events—although those exist, too.

Everyone Has 10 Minutes per Week to Learn

TOP EXECUTIVES ALWAYS TALK ABOUT the importance of being a "learning organization." Very few of them can explain how they're doing it, and some are surprised when they find out they aren't.

For example, a multi-national company had 10,000 English-speaking employees who needed training. They contracted with a major e-learning vendor to provide over 1,000 off-the-shelf training programs on nearly every topic imaginable. Departments were notified that this training was available, and employees were told that they could take courses as needed as part of the enterprise licensing agreement.

This was considered by the Training department to be a major component of the organization's overall employee development solution and was presented to the folks at the big table as such. The message to management was, "Our training needs are covered. We have this extensive inventory of e-learning programs available from one of the leading vendors."

At the end of the contract year, everyone was surprised to discover that the total number of individual courses completed by the 10,000 person employee pool was 200. The Training department wanted to keep offering the programs because they filled major holes in Training's content lineup, and the vendor wanted to keep the licensing revenue. So the 200 number was swept under the rug and the contract was extended.

To be fair, there could be a number of possible reasons for the low usage number. The courses were classic click-and-read style, so they weren't particularly engrossing. No customized Level 2 programs had been developed to support the generic content. Perhaps the course availability could have been better communicated across the organization. Even so, only 200 courses were completed by 10,000 employees? Important lessons can be learned from this.

Learning is not a course.

You saw it in the previous chapter. Learning is not a course; it's a process. This organization, like many others, failed to integrate the third-party off-the-shelf training into its overall employee development system. Without that linkage, training was just an "OK-to-do" activity rather than a "need-to-do" requirement.

Having too many training options can be overwhelming.

As impressive as it is to tell management that there are thousands of programs available, this number is a barrier to prospective learners. Workers with a training need have to go through a time-consuming process merely to find something that might help them. They must review the entire course inventory from a list of thousands of candidates, identify individual titles that may apply, read those course descriptions, and then view enough of the program to see if they have made the right selection. Plus, their managers don't know how to advise them because they're confused, too.

People do not need thousands of courses.

Like most work situations, the 80-20 Rule is alive and well with training. You can assume that a core set of 20% of the training is going to deliver about 80% of the benefits. The remaining topics might be nice to know, but they're not going to move the payback needle in a major way.

Because most people have already had lots of training, the tendency is to want to offer advanced or secondary training courses. Yet all you have to do is listen to front-line workers and you'll hear why things continue to go wrong. It always ends up being the fundamentals—the "blocking and tackling" of daily work—topics such as leadership, supervision, communication, motivation, personal productivity, safety, and HR compliance. Make certain that everyone is competent in those areas, and watch what happens to performance.

Improvement requires a curriculum.

If organizations want to continuously improve their productivity, then they must have a process in place to raise performance standards and teach workers how to meet them. This means that learners must be given a formal curriculum to complete that is fully supported by the overall training process.

One organization created an internal "college" consisting of seven-year curricula for critical job titles. Employees were expected to obtain their bachelors, masters, and Ph.D. "degrees" by completing a comprehensive performance improvement curriculum that was offered in addition to their basic job training.

The curricula consisted of a set of targeted Level 1 off-the-shelf training programs supplemented by custom Level 2 programs applying those skills to specific job requirements in their industry. The organization used this to formally raise the bar on performance standards year by year.

Make learning a part of the job.

With a formal curriculum in place, you can then establish with workers that they are expected to learn. They need to understand that training is not something that takes them away from their job. It's a part of their job.

Make learning a regular activity.

Training cannot be a periodic event. As we saw in Chapter 3.4, single event training doesn't work. Learning has to become a habit, a regular task.

Managers will counter that their people don't have time for frequent training. And that's true if you're talking about traditional classroom or CBT programs. But the response to that objection is simple.

Everyone has 10 minutes per week to learn.

As part of the expectation that it's everyone's job to learn, you must also establish that formal training is something that is done every week. Again, that's the beauty of short-form media such as video that can be deployed to the six screens. Training can take place anywhere, such as at a weekly team meeting or during a few dead minutes in the day.

Using this approach, every employee completes 50 programs in a curriculum each year, *for the rest of their career.* The training can be a mix of new programs to introduce improvement skills and refresh learning reviews of past programs. But either way, the learning is continuous.

This is how to become a learning organization. Training is integrated into weekly work schedules and covers formal curricula that continue to improve worker productivity and results over time. Otherwise, you're going to be paying for 1,000+ programs and having only 200 program completions across a population of 10,000 potential students … with no needles moving anywhere.

▷ To Do

To become a learning organization, a number of questions need answering. It starts with taking a long-range view of training in the context of the organization's goals.

1. What are your organization's strategic initiatives? What skills need to be in place to achieve them over time? What is it going to require to improve the workforce in order to attain them? How long is that going to take? What are the annual training goals that lead to success with those initiatives?

2. What jobs have the key leverage? What new or improved skills will they require?

3. How do those skills get broken up into curricula over time? What are the goals for the first year? The second year? … and so on.

4. Does the Training department have a short-form training process in place that can support regular training? If not, how can that be developed?

5. How does training become integrated into the weekly workflow? Into the overall training process?

In order to continuously improve workplace performance, learning must become a regular activity. Everyone has 10 minutes per week to learn. It's your job to provide that training.

6.4

The Manager's Role
in the Learning Process

TRAINERS HAVE ALL HAD STUDENTS TELL THEM, "The first thing my boss asked me after I got back from class was, 'What did you learn?'" Managers are either curious or else feel a bit threatened by having subordinates know something that they don't.

This would be funny if it wasn't so disturbing. The ASTD study from Chapter 6.1 found that a primary cause of failures in transfer of learning is managers who don't reinforce newly trained behaviors. That's why manager coaching is a critical phase in the overall worker training process.

We discovered this the hard way with some training for commercial loan officers. The goal was to teach them how to negotiate for better terms and conditions in a very competitive environment. Customers were actively shopping lenders for the best rates that also required the least collateral. The needles to be moved were a measurable improvement in loan yields and a reduction in losses from defaults.

The training itself was very successful. Loan officers went back to their branches all fired up to negotiate with customers and use all the strategies they had learned.

It was to be expected that some loan opportunities would naturally be lost in the negotiation. This was seen by top management as a good thing. Loan officers would be obtaining better rates and writing more secure loans. Executives were happy to see high-risk loans go to competitors. But that's not how the branch managers saw it. They were focused on loan volume. The first time that their branch lost a prospect due to negotiating, they made sure to express their strong displeasure to the offending loan officer. It became immediately clear to loan officers that negotiating was simply a great way to get in trouble with their boss, and they never again negotiated anything. The result was that no needles moved, and the training was a complete waste of time.

We quickly learned that if a financial institution didn't plan to include the branch managers in the training, then we should decline the engagement. It was destined for failure.

Branch managers needed to go through not only the entire negotiations training program alongside their loan officers but also attend a separate session. This one included a discussion of leadership's commitment to the new strategy, and it provided special training on how to coach and reinforce the new negotiating skills.

In addition, the organization had to expand the way branch managers were evaluated from a pure volume measure to include average yield and net cost of defaults. In other words, leaders had to address all the phases of the training process.

With these additional elements in place, financial institutions began to see measurable improvements in yield and loan security, and negotiating skills became a standard part of their commercial loan officer training requirements.

In addition to coaching information, some topics have associated content that should be given separately to managers. For example, assume that you have a Diversity Training series that is mandatory for all employees. Research shows that standalone diversity training doesn't work. It can actually generate a backlash, and mandatory training may even activate biases.[1] There are some steps that can help organizations manage diversity, but they focus on what is going on outside of the training. This is sensitive content that should be shared exclusively with managers if a diversity training initiative is to be effective.

The research is clear. Managers are a critical leverage point for trainers. Their involvement in personnel development is a must-have, yet they're often totally ignored. Yes, there might be a supervisory or management skills curriculum. It could even include a generic sequence on coaching skills. But those courses are about managers' own personal development.

You need to make certain that managers are prepared to support their subordinates upon returning from training. Managers also need any additional information that's important to the organization, but that was not part of the employee program.

Managers need to know what's being taught. They need to understand how to debrief employees on what was learned during the training. They need suggestions on how to deal with the learning curve until new skills are mastered, as well as what to do if an employee struggles. They need to understand the measures used to track employee performance in these new skills, what achievement levels to expect, and what possible reinforcement or rewards can be provided.

For example, in the "10-minutes-per-week" system, managers actually complete two curricula. The first would be their own supervisory or management curriculum. The second would be their subordinates' curricula, which need to be completed in a week-ahead fashion. In other words, managers are always taking the same training their people are taking, except they are doing it a week in advance so that they can discuss it during the next team meeting and coach to it on an individual basis. This way there will never be a "What did you learn in training?" question.

So you need to have management courses focused on the organizational issues surrounding training and on how to coach the specific skills taught. Otherwise, how can you expect managers to add any value to the learning process?

▷ To Do

This requires a major shift in thinking for organizations that have been focused solely on the immediate learner.

1. Evaluate the role of managers in your training process. As we discussed in Chapter 2.1, are managers considered customers of training? Or do you assume that the actual transfer of learning is somebody else's problem?

2. Review your existing set of training programs. Do you have titles such as "Coaching for Key Account Sales Training" or "Leadership Issues in Employee Engagement" or "How to Use the DISC Training Series" in the list? Just like Diversity, many topics often require further management training.
3. Consider the issue of specialized management content and specific coaching techniques early in your development cycle. Plan on creating that additional content when warranted.
4. Educate managers on how to use these targeted "apply" training programs designed especially for them.
5. Educate middle managers on the new level of involvement for managers in the front-line training process. Make certain that the targeted programs are added to supervisory and management curricula and that middle managers are following up on that training in a week-ahead fashion, just like supervisors are following up on front-line training.

Managers asking "What did you learn today?" are admitting that they are ill-prepared to coach on what you're teaching their subordinates. If you truly intend to move the needle with training, then you must involve managers in the subordinate training process.

Train First, Then Promote

MANY ORGANIZATIONS PROVIDE TRAINING exactly backwards from the way employees actually need it. A good example is how supervisors are initially trained.

New supervisors often struggle right after they're promoted. The general consensus is that supervision is an extremely difficult job, and moving from front-line worker to workgroup leader is one of the biggest transitions employees may face in their entire career.

There's a lot of truth to this. Going from buddy to boss creates some tricky interpersonal dynamics with former co-workers. Supervision requires a very different set of skills versus front-line work. And the workload is suddenly more intense as new supervisors go from worrying about a single job to making sure an entire workgroup is performing well.

So how do organizations address this? Without any preliminaries, they promote front-line workers into the job and let them struggle for a few weeks or months. Then they send them to a high-intensity "New Manager School" for a week or two where they're buried with all sorts of totally new information. (See Chapter 5.2 on meetings.). Finally, there may be an "Advanced Manager's School" to attend after another six months or so.

This is not anticipation learning. It's catch-up learning. It's like tossing non-swimmers into the deep end of the pool and telling them they'll get some swimming lessons in a few months. In the meantime, just try to keep their heads above water.

Look at this experience from the viewpoint of new supervisors. They were great at what they used to do, so management decided to promote them to something they don't know how to do. They're trying to pick up where the previous supervisor left off, learn the intricacies of the new job, get to know their new subordinates, and not have anything blow up in their face. And the complete training on how to do all this may be a year away. It's no wonder they're panicked.

Now contrast this with how the fire department trains leaders. It doesn't promote firemen to captain and then start training them afterwards. This is a life-and-death job. A burning building is not the place for mistakes to be made because a new captain hasn't yet received the proper training.

Candidates for captain have to pass a Fire Captain Written Exam along with meeting other qualification requirements. Passing this test doesn't automatically make them a captain. It puts them on the list of "eligible to be promoted." They have now been judged ready to perform the job of fire captain *before* getting the position.

Organizations can learn a lesson from this approach. Instead of training people after they get a job, how about training them beforehand so that they can be immediately productive?

Imagine that you have a front-line employee whom you think would make a good supervisor. You talk about it during her performance review and suggest that she complete the supervisor curriculum program. Upon passing that, she'll be put on the "ready" list for potential supervisors. New supervisors are picked only from this list. Makes sense, right? Not to everybody.

There are two common objections to training for qualification. The first response is that this is a perfect example of anticipation learning, where the new skills will be forgotten long before she gets the promotion. That might be true for skills such as *Excel* commands. But supervisory training is about general operations and soft skills. Training in advance delivers a number of advantages.

Career development. One of the hardest parts of the appraisal form for managers to fill out is the Career Development section. Employees want to know what they can do to better themselves and move their careers forward. Oftentimes, there is nothing they can do but wait. Qualification training lets employees proactively improve their skills and position themselves for advancement. Completing the curriculum for a new job doesn't guarantee a promotion. But not completing it guarantees there will never be a promotion.

Motivation. Qualification training provides a good test for workers. Almost everyone wants to move up the ladder and earn more money, but many employees aren't really willing to work for it. This way you find out if a candidate has the internal motivation to finish the training in order to become a supervisor. If not, then this person isn't someone you want for a leader.

Exposure. This gives candidates an early taste of what being a supervisor entails. Some candidates will be fascinated and challenged. Some will realize that supervision is not for them and drop out of the process. Either way, it's a win-win for both the employee and the organization.

Perspective. An old tip on how to get a promotion is to start thinking like your boss. Adopt the same viewpoints. Talk about the same issues. Use the same vocabulary. Analyze things from the same outlook. Supervisor training expands employees' perspective to a more global view of the bigger issues. They will start thinking like their bosses, which is never a bad thing.

Productivity. Supervisory training need not be forgotten over time, particularly if the employee's manager starts coaching those skills. The soft skills are useful at any level of employment. And the operational skills can only make employees better coaches and team leaders until they're actually promoted. So there are plenty of "apply" opportunities, even for front-line workers.

The second common objection is that it's costly and impractical to train employees on jobs they don't currently have. It seems like a wasted expense if they are not promoted or if they're promoted into a different job. This is a valid concern, but it's one that's easily handled. This is one more reason why organizations have gone to short-form e-learning models for the majority of their training needs. With an existing supervisory training curriculum already online, there is a minimal marginal cost in having additional employees complete the training.

There is the cost of the training time itself, but you have seen that it can be delivered in 10-minute blocks and is shorter than the equivalent classroom training. So the disruption in productivity is minimal. Everyone has 10 minutes per week to learn.

We've focused on supervisory training, but the fire department model works for any job and in any industry. Instead of training novices for jobs they already have and don't know how to do, you can train people for positions they aspire to. This will make them better employees until they are promoted.

◗ **To Do**

This is an opportunity for the Training department to get involved with existing performance management processes in the organization.

1. Review your organization's promotion practices and the timing of the associated training. Are you post-training or pre-training (or not training at all)?
2. Meet with HR to discuss how you can help support a competency qualification effort.
3. Choose a possible promotion (supervision is an ideal one) to use in evaluating the benefits of pre-training.

You need to make certain that everyone, no matter how new in their job, is ready to perform to standards. Pre-training is a way to do that, as well as to also improve employee performance in current jobs prior to a promotion.

6.6

From Blended Learning to Multi-Purposed Learning

IN ACQUISITION LEARNING, the general consensus among trainers has been that there is a requirement for more than one medium. Most believe that some content lends itself for conversion to e-learning, and some content is still taught better face-to-face. For example, it's assumed that e-learning works well with technical skills and classroom learning works best with soft skills.

This gave rise to the idea of *blended learning.* An agreed-upon formal definition of the term doesn't exist. In general, it's a philosophy of teaching a subject using a mixture of modalities. This can include combining classroom, e-learning, online meetings, tutoring, mentoring, social media, and so on.

A typical example is a leading technology company that wanted to convert its annual week-long product introduction and training conference into a 2-day meeting. The decision was to move the new product features training to pre-work CBT and then focus the meeting on sales applications and prospecting for each product line. There was no product training in the meeting, no sales training in the pre-work, and no post-event activities at all.

Blended learning is essentially this act of division. It requires breaking up content and determining how each part is going to be taught. There is usually no overlap of information across modes. Each has its own separate purpose. The blended programs then provide the complete message.

This is what we call a "create-many, deploy-once" approach. Blended learning helps reduce the high costs of in-person training, but any one medium provides only a partial solution.

As you saw in Chapter 5.1, it's not a matter of figuring out what portion of classroom content can be converted to e-learning without a loss in effectiveness. It's the exact opposite. The question is what portion of the e-learning content absolutely requires classroom training above and beyond the coaching that managers provide.

A much better alternative is to establish a "create-once, deploy-many" approach in which a single training program is used multiple ways. This minimizes both delivery costs and development costs for acquisition training. We call this approach *multi-purposed learning*. The question is how to do it.

One of the big advantages of building training curricula around an e-learning structure such as short-form video is that it enables a multi-purposed learning strategy, with all the benefits that entails. A single video training program can be used for:

Initial learning. You've seen the research showing the advantages of short-form video as an acquisition training medium and how it can be designed in accordance with the research on adult learning.

Refresh learning. The same holds true for the retention phase. Short-form video is an excellent refresh learning medium that facilitates quick access to specific content in a non-linear fashion.

Manager coaching. As one supervisor put it, "I'm not a good trainer, but I know the job and I'm a good coach." Short-form video allows managers to have permanent access to the original instructor giving the training perfectly. A manager can sit down with a subordinate after a ride-along and have this type of coaching conversation at the end of the day:

"Remember the objection that tripped you up at Billy Bob's Burger Barn? That was a Misunderstanding objection. Let's go back and look at how you could have handled that. (Drag the video slider to the right spot and a show a short clip from the Handling Objections series.) Now what should you have said there?"

Team meetings. Managers are always looking for short training bits to use at a team meeting. They can show a 10-minute video, have a quick discussion on how to apply that today, and then continue their meeting. This is an ideal approach to address the "10-minutes-per-week-to-learn" curriculum.

Performance support. The entire video, or individual clips from it, can be deployed to mobile devices to be used for guidance right before doing a task.

The key point to understand is that *all five of these functions use the same training video.* Rather than five different training programs in different mediums, each used one way, there is one training program used five different ways—without any other specialized development for the additional uses.

Now, instead of moving portions of classroom teaching into e-learning in a blended approach and perhaps ignoring functions such as refresh learning or performance support, you are providing a comprehensive solution with just a single training deliverable.

Instead of generating marginal cost improvements for training, you're generating transformational reductions in cost—all while actually increasing the functionality and reach of your training. You are creating once and deploying many with a multi-purposed learning strategy.

◗ **To Do**
Blended learning needs to give way to multi-purposed learning.
1. Stop thinking that instructional design is initially a decision about where to put each block of content in a blended approach.

2. Recognize that truly compelling training needs to be deployed for a variety of uses to ensure the success of the initial learning event, coaching for transfer of learning, and long-term retention of content.
3. Create training solutions that can be easily used beyond the initial learning event in the overall training process. That means they have to be short and deployed anywhere.

You saw in Chapter 5.8 why Cisco's John Chambers called video the "killer app" of the Internet and said that it would be used in different forms as part of a unified communications strategy. Now you see another reason why. When training content can be multi-purposed, the overall benefits to organizations are enormous.

How to Pilot a Training Program

PART 6 HAS BEEN ALL ABOUT changing the way you operate—using the research we covered in Parts 3 and 4 to transform training into something that moves the needle on business results and creates a rapid payback. You understand it now and see how it needs to be done, but you may be the only person in your organization who does.

The research may be sufficient for you to become a believer, but proof from the outside, no matter how credible it is, may still not be enough for your executive decision makers. They insist on seeing it for themselves, right in the organization, no matter how many expert opinions you assemble and studies you quote. That is when it's time to conduct a pilot program.

The purpose of a pilot is to test the application of these concepts, not to prove them at a fundamental level. This is an important expectation to set. Then it's a matter of conducting a pilot that will generate the measures you need to make a decision on the training. Here's a process for getting that information:

1. Determine measures for the pilot.

Training must drive business results. With a short pilot, often there is not enough time for training to generate measurable outcomes. All you have is testing plus learner and manager feedback (Kirkpatrick Levels 1 through 3). Questions you can ask managers are:

- Did the training meet its goals?
- Do your subordinates use it on the job?

- Did it help them in some way? How?
- Would you recommend the organization implement this training?

Questions you can ask learners are:
- Did you complete the training?
- Did it use your time efficiently?
- Did you consider it useful?
- Did you use it on the job?
- Did it help you in some way? How?
- Would you recommend the organization implement this training?

2. Determine the length of the pilot.

You want evaluators to have enough time to complete sample training, but you don't want to stretch the pilot over too long a time. For e-learning, 30 days is a common pilot timeframe—long enough to complete sample courses and apply them, but not too long to lose focus on the process. A core skills training pilot may take longer, perhaps up to 60 or 90 days.

3. Select evaluators.

The evaluators need to reflect your ultimate user base as closely as possible and should consist of employees who are interested in personal development. Select several evaluators from all levels of the organization—leadership, management, supervision, front-line—and across relevant departments. You're looking for people who will not only complete the training but also be concerned about organizational improvement and possess sufficient evaluation skills to be insightful reviewers.

4. Create assignments and timelines for evaluators.

If it's an online pilot, assign courses for evaluators on the basis of their individual positions. Evaluators should complete the training in the first half of the pilot so that they can spend the remaining time implementing the new skills they've learned. Also encourage evaluators to explore other titles that interest them.

5. Roll out the pilot.

For online training, conduct a formal rollout event, such as a webcast or conference call. Explain the pilot's goals, everyone's assignments, how to access the training, and the questions they'll be asked at the end of the pilot (see #1). Remind them to download any student materials and to always take the post-tests.

   For classroom pilots, make certain to set your expectations at the start of the program. Then allow extra time to discuss the pilot itself throughout the program.

6. Monitor the online pilot.

At the midpoint of the online pilot, contact any evaluators who have not yet accessed the training. Find out if there are technical issues, and remind them to complete their assignments. At the same time, recognize that this reluctance to complete the training is feedback in and of itself, especially if the participant took a program or two and then stopped. That could indicate that the training content is not compelling.

7. Review the pilot usage logs.

At the end of the pilot period, verify that evaluators have completed their training and post-training assignments and did so with enough time to actually apply some of the new skills on the job. It's the only way to ensure that your results are valid.

8. Survey the evaluators.

Start your review with quantitative feedback. You can use simple web-based tools to create an online survey. In addition to the questions in #1, you can also ask about the value of the student materials and post-tests, along with any other topics of concern.

9. Conduct phone interviews.

For qualitative feedback, conduct short phone interviews with a representative subset of evaluators. Make sure to interview managers of selected evaluators to see if the manager saw any changed behavior.

How many people do you interview after the pilot? You'll know your research is done when you reach "closure" (i.e., when you no longer hear anything new during interviews).

10. Make the recommendation.
The pilot will provide user data on the projected effectiveness of the online training being evaluated. This can then be used in your overall evaluation of training alternatives.

◎ To Do
Here are some specific tips for getting the most out of this pilot process:
1. Be alert to the fact that employees may not want any training at all. This could be because they have had a bad experience with training in the past or as the saying goes, "they don't know what they don't know." Perhaps they're simply resistant to change. When training is an organizational imperative, evaluators need to understand that they're being asked to help make this the best training, not to approve or veto this training overall.
2. In assigning online courses for a pilot, pick one or two that everyone takes and then assign the remaining courses on the basis of individual positions and job levels. This will provide both standardized and job-related course feedback.
3. If any of the evaluators "crammed" to complete their assignments right before the pilot deadline, you need to remove them from the post-pilot evaluation because they had no time to actually apply any of the training on the job. All they can give you is satisfaction feedback on their course experience, and that isn't enough.

Pilots are a great way to make your business case for training. They allow management to make a smaller, preliminary commitment to training, and they give you the data you need for a proof source.

Part 7

The Future for Training

THE TRAINING FUNCTION is in the midst of a major transition. For years, trainers created classic sit-and-learn programs using classroom or CBT methods. Now learning is a mobile and social process using new media and different delivery modes.

This is unsettling for many trainers, especially those with significant experience in the industry. The role of the Training department seems to be diminishing, and the skills that have made trainers successful in the past no longer seem to offer the same value.

It's not that there is a shrinking role for Training departments. But there is certainly a *different* role for trainers in the coming years. This new role presents enormous opportunities for Training to become a more strategic partner with top leadership.

In Part 1, we talked about two classic questions that trainers regularly ask:

How do I get management to value training?
How do I get people to take training?

We have addressed those in depth throughout the book. Now we need to answer a third classic question:

What is the future of training?

A New Role for Training

WE'RE OLD ENOUGH TO REMEMBER having an administrative assistant who would write our letters. All we had to do was identify the addressee, jot down the main points to cover, and back came a beautifully written and formatted letter on company stationery. Then came the word processing center where we had to write the letter completely on our own and someone would type it up on a primitive memory typewriter with a tiny screen. With the advent of personal computers, we had to start doing our own letters, and with the addition of e-mail the self-producing nature of correspondence was complete.

This same transition took place with document layout and presentation slides. We used to write the copy and hand it in to the experts in the graphics department. Then we began doing it ourselves with desktop publishing and presentation programs on our PCs, with predictably amateurish results. Although we ultimately got better at it, we were never going to be as good as the graphics artists. But we could at least produce professional work.

The same thing is now happening with video. We originally had to go to an ad agency or a production studio to create video, and the costs could exceed $1,000 per minute. It required a studio, super-expensive equipment, and a group of highly trained specialists in direction, camera operations, lighting, sound, makeup, and editing.

Next came prosumer video, which allowed anybody to use digital cameras and edit the video on regular PCs. Although perhaps not up to broadcast TV standards, the quality was fine for workplace uses. So once again it was amateur hour, only this time for video production.

Today, consumer devices are starting to include video capture and video chat capabilities as standard features. At this point, as long as they have a phone, anyone located anywhere can be a video producer (as many celebrities have found out to their embarrassment). Many examples of amateurish videos are out there, but they're out there. Boy, are they ever out there!

As this is being written, 48 hours of video are uploaded to YouTube every minute, which is 8 years of content uploaded daily. This is the equivalent of 240,000 full-length movies uploaded every week. More content is uploaded in a month than the three major TV networks have created in 60 years. On the viewing side, there are 3 billion YouTube views per day, and over 1 trillion views per year.[1]

We're not trying to pound this to death. The point is that video is here to stay in the consumer space. But what's puzzling to workers (and customers) is why video adoption has been so slow to take hold in the workplace and why there is so little support for it. As we discussed in Chapter 5.8, everyone agrees that video definitely works better.

One good thing about all this consumer action is that people no longer expect video to be an expensive production extravaganza. Starting with early TV shows using hand-held camera techniques and continuing with the explosion of reality TV shows, viewers have come to accept bad video. Still, it's one thing to use home-grown video in a professional fashion. It's another to use it and look amateurish.

Left to their own devices, people are still at the self-production stage like they were when they were churning out terrible letters, ransom-note-styled desktop publishing documents, and horrible slides—only now it's video. Someone has to show learners how to effectively utilize video and to create higher-quality video content when it is called for.

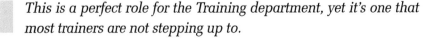

This is a perfect role for the Training department, yet it's one that most trainers are not stepping up to.

The production of professional video media is well outside many trainers' comfort zone. For most organizations, the use of video for training has been at both ends of the spectrum. It has meant setting a video camera up on a tripod in the corner of the room and taping a session, or it has meant engaging a video producer for a full-blown studio or on-site shoot with all the bells and whistles.

At one end, it is horrible video. A wide classroom shot. Poor lighting. Tinny audio. At the other end, it is expensive overkill that drains the Training department's budget. Consequently, video has not hit the mainstream with Training, much less become the de facto medium for communication across the enterprise, which is what the pundits are suggesting is going to happen.

The Training department is the recognized expert in packaging content for effective transfer of knowledge. By not stepping up to the video revolution currently taking place, Training is going to permanently cede this strategic role to some other department such as communications or HR, or even to the various operational departments.

By stepping up, we mean that Training needs to develop competencies in the unique instructional design and production requirements of video content. Video-based programs have very different standards than do classroom and traditional e-learning programs.

Training needs to establish an in-house or outsourced production capability. This has to support a rapid development and deployment process in order to generate the advantages in time-to-market of information and skills we talked about in Chapter 2.3.

Trainers need to expand their skills. We've seen experienced instructors who consistently generate top scores on smile sheets totally freeze up in a studio. We've seen presenters unable to generate any energy talking to a camera lens versus speaking to live bodies. We've seen trainers unable to read a script with conviction, or lose their place on the teleprompter as they look from screen to screen. Video production is a new training process requiring a very different set of professional skills.

Finally, Training must establish itself as the packaging expert for video-based content. You need to be the go-to source across the entire extended enterprise for help with video. That's the way to secure your very existence in this Web 2.0 media world.

◑ To Do
If you're not there already, then it's time to get on the video bandwagon.
1. Begin educating the entire Training department on the instructional design differences required for video-based content.
2. Develop the new set of presenter skills needed to deliver training in a video format.
3. Create training programs to help other departments get the most out of their home-grown video efforts.
4. Insist on video-based content from third-party training vendors. Require that it meet your instructional design standards.
5. Develop the capability for video production. This could be either an in-house facility or a partnership with an outsourced vendor. Either way, the processes used must support a short time to market for video-based content.
6. Promote your services across the enterprise. Departments are likely using a variety of vendors to assist them with traditional video production. You can do it faster, cheaper, and better.

The handwriting is on the wall. It's not a matter of whether or not you are going to use video. It's a matter of *when* and *how* you're going to use it to move your organization's scorecard needles. This is a great opportunity to expand the value and reach of the Training department.

Transferring Intellectual Capital to the Next Generation

SOME YEARS AGO a major manufacturer decided to cut 10% of its workforce across the board. In addition to a large severance payout, it allowed long-term employees to add five years to their age and five years to their employment time in calculating early retirement benefits. As you can imagine, a large number of experienced employees voluntarily took the exit package.

The result was a headhunter feeding frenzy. The company's main competitors flooded the city with recruiters and cherry-picked the best of the former employees. One of the recruiters commented, "We couldn't believe it. Their management essentially said, 'Let's pay our most experienced employees to go over to our competitors.' We could never have enticed these people to leave on their own."

It was a double hit. Not only did the manufacturer give its competitors talent that it had spent decades developing, but the company and industry knowledge that those employees possessed walked out the door with little notice ahead of time. All that knowledge was gone forever.

This whole concept leads to another one of those questions that leaves leaders with a blank look on their faces:

"What is your plan to transfer knowledge from experienced workers on the way out to new workers coming in?"

According to *The Conference Board,* "Despite both the risk and cost of losing intellectual capital, most companies still have no plan for the management and transfer of knowledge, and even fewer factor cross-generational challenges into business strategy."[1]

The real issue isn't layoffs, although that certainly is a big one. The major issue beginning right now is the transfer of expertise between generations of workers. Here's what you face.

The baby boom continues to affect society in the United States. As the population bubble begins to age out of the workplace, organizations are facing an unprecedented and permanent loss of institutional knowledge. Literally decades of experience are walking out the door as older workers head into retirement or are laid off for whatever reasons.

- The fastest growing age group in the labor force is workers 45 and older.[2]
- An estimated 79 million Baby Boomers (born between 1946 and 1964) will be leaving the workforce in the coming years.[3]
- For the next 19 years, over 10,000 Baby Boomers will reach age 65 *every day.*[4]
- Although younger employees are coming in, the supply of key talent will decrease by 15% over the next 15 years while demand will increase by 25%.[5]

In addition, the learning preferences of people in their 20s are very different than those in their 50s.

Twenty-somethings are comfortable with technology. They need to be busy. Social media and collaboration is a way of life. They are multi-taskers and information junkies.

Fifty-somethings have talent, knowledge, and experience. They have significant business acumen gained over a lifetime, but they're less comfortable with technology and social media.

The first message for trainers is that their organization needs to develop a formal strategy for the transfer of knowledge between generations.

The second message is that the traditional classroom and CBT programs developed through the years for fifty-somethings are not going to cut it with the twenty-somethings. As we have discussed throughout the book, organizations can't keep ignoring the realities of adult learning or, in this case, the requirements of younger adult learning.

Becoming the owner of the generational knowledge transfer process is an ideal job for the Training department. Look at the steps *The Conference Board* details:

1. Identify and evaluate the knowledge.
2. Validate and document the knowledge.
3. Publish and share the knowledge.
4. Transfer and apply the knowledge.
5. Learn and capture the knowledge.

This is exactly what you do well. The Training department is perfectly positioned for these tasks.

Taking on this job is also a great way to transition from a tactical manufacturer of education into a strategic partner helping management leverage critical institutional knowledge. Organizations have made a strong business case for the effort and have generated measurable hard-dollar benefits. For example, *Fortune* estimates that it costs organizations $50,000 to $100,000 to lose a professional employee, and losing key talent costs even more.[6]

The knowledge transfer process is also another way to expand the role of the Training department. Not every solution involves training. For example, organizations are experimenting with formal programs where mentors are matched up with protégés using a very structured methodology. Facilitating this process is another ideal role for the Training department.

Trainers can't afford to take a wait-and-see attitude on this. The retirement exodus is starting now and will be a fact of life for the next two decades. It's clear from the research that:

- Organizations need a comprehensive knowledge transfer methodology that takes content, technology, and generational differences into account.
- The process needs to be in operation *before* people are ready to walk out the door.
- Knowledge transfer is not an event. It needs to be part of everyday processes.

- The younger generation needs to be involved in the project design and management.
- A hard-dollar payback for the effort will need to be identified.

This is not yet a disaster situation. Employees have been retiring ever since people have been working. It's just that there have never been so many experienced employees retiring at one time. This creates a need over the next 19 years for someone to handle the transfer of information to the next generation. That presents the Training department with a substantial opportunity to become strategically important to the organization. It's an opportunity that cannot be missed.

◗ To Do

You need to help your organization manage its institutional knowledge just like it does any other asset.

1. Assess your organization. Do you already have a knowledge transfer process in place? Are you studying the problem? Or are you generating blank looks when you ask about it?
2. Do your homework on this issue. What information can you find publicly on it? What are best practices in your locale? In your industry?
3. Build a preliminary plan. You don't want to be in a position of bringing up the issue, then being asked what you recommend and not having an answer.
4. Start laying the groundwork. Put together a management briefing and include why the Training department is perfectly positioned to own this process. By being the first to bring it up, you have the best chance of being asked to address it.

They say that in hours you can learn how a machine works, but it takes years to be able to listen to one and tell what's wrong. If things don't change, this is the type of knowledge that will be lost as experienced employees move on. Training needs to be deeply involved in the capture and transfer of departing expertise. This is a strategic opportunity that Training can't afford to pass up.

Building a Framework for Execution

AS WE CONTINUE TO LOOK AT WAYS to expand your value proposition to management, there's another opportunity that has enormous, enterprise-wide strategic potential for Training departments.

A hot topic in the IT world right now is *unified communications.* You first saw this term used in Chapter 5.8 by John Chambers in his assessment of video.

Organizations are faced with a confusing mashup of various communications technologies such as phone, voicemail, text messaging, fax, e-mail, instant messaging, audio and video conferencing, and webcasting. The goal of a unified communications architecture is to develop a set of products that present a consistent user interface across multiple devices and media types. Although everyone is talking about it, the initiative is currently in the early stages, and implementations are partial at best.

It's important to recognize that this is only the technology side of unified communications. What Chambers referred to, and what no one else is talking about, is the *content* side of unified communications, which is in similar disarray.

Think about the situation. Today's work environment is an information tsunami. Some SMEs have critical institutional knowledge. Then there are constituencies who need that information. But it's not like there is no communication going on. SMEs are churning out all kinds of content, and constituencies are getting it from all directions. This causes two problems.

First, organizations are spending massive and unrecognized amounts of money on a fragmented effort at communication and training. They are using three ad agencies, 15 commercial printers, 20 different training vendors—duplications that go on and on. No one knows the true enterprise cost for all this because it's spread across various departmental budgets. No single Chart of Account bucket, where all these expenses are accumulated, exists.

Second, no one is happy. It's ironic. SMEs are complaining that people aren't listening to them. Constituents are complaining that even though they are getting buried with information, they are still not getting what they really need to be successful.

We've dubbed this "The Great Divide." People have information that other people want, but it's not getting transferred in a way that's useful. This disconnect prevents organizations from being nimble and effective.

What's needed is a comprehensive, enterprise-wide *Framework for Execution* to handle the dissemination of information and skills across the organization. This is both a content and media capability that utilizes an organization's unified communications IT architecture. The results are dramatically lower costs of communication and learning and a strategic competitive advantage in time to market of information and skills.

As Chambers pointed out, the "killer" medium for unified communications is short-form video. Video has higher receptivity among constituents, increases retention, and is proven to move the needle on business results. Video becomes the universal connection among SMEs, content, and constituents.

For organizations to be effective, someone needs to manage the enterprise-wide knowledge transfer process. Someone needs to help SMEs select information, package it, and send it where it needs to go. Someone needs to set priorities and measure results.

This is where the Training department comes in to bridge the divide. As workers with digital age mobile devices become self-contained content producers, this is where the Training department can add value.

Figure 7.3.1 shows an example Framework for the subsidiary of a multi-national holding company. The column on the left represents the various SMEs who have information. The column on the right represents the range of constituents who need information. The middle column represents the content to be shared. The bridge between the three columns is the Training department.

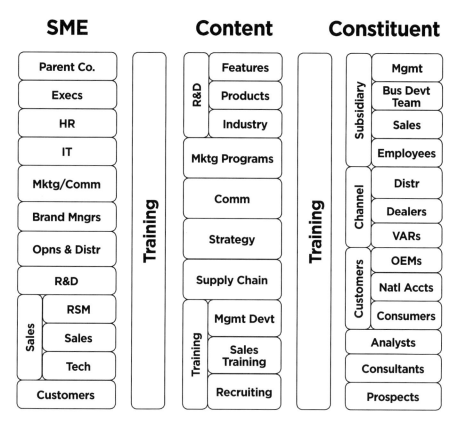

Figure 7.3.1. Example Framework for Execution

In implementing its Framework, this organization prioritized which "connections" it would create according to the organization's strategic goals. Its immediate needles were share growth and supply chain efficiency. So in the first year, it focused on providing marketing program information to customers and the sales channel, sales training to employees and channel partners, and distribution process training to channel partners.

Implementing a Framework of Execution is a rare win-win situation in which organizations can reduce costs and actually *increase* effectiveness. Creating a unified communication and training architecture using short-form video allows an organization to consolidate its efforts around a single content technology. This not only eliminates duplication and waste through centralization and standardization but also improves the quality and effectiveness of the content itself.

The result is a fundamental strategic role for the Training department across the entire enterprise. It also offers the opportunity to actually increase budget allocations for Training because a portion of actual cost savings from other departments can be transferred to the Training department for use in implementing the Framework.

◗ To Do

This is the other half of the unified communications initiative, and it is a different way of looking at knowledge transfer within your organization.

1. Find out where your IT department is in the implementation of a unified communications architecture. This isn't required to implement a Framework, but it can be helpful if you can piggyback on the effort.
2. Unified communications is normally considered to be solely a technology issue. Point out to management that the effort is only a partial answer and that there has to be a similar architecture in place for content in order to have a complete solution. Otherwise, it's like buying a fast car and not having any people to take somewhere quickly.
3. Run a planning meeting to develop a Framework map like the one in Figure 7.3.1.
4. Prioritize an implementation—who is connecting to whom concerning what content. A three-year planning horizon seems to work well.

Content creation is clearly moving into the mainstream, where every worker can be a publishing SME. We believe that implementing a video-based Framework for Execution is the most important opportunity available for Training departments to establish and expand their value to top management. This is literally a one-time chance to put Training at the heart of operations across the organization and ensure your continued success and your department's funding.

Training in a Dysfunctional Organization

WE ONCE ASKED a manufacturer's staff if they had a sales channel training program for their extensive and complex product line. They said that they had a single full-time dealer training manager who visited stores nationwide on a periodic basis. When we finally met him, we asked how often he saw each dealer because they numbered in the thousands. He said he visited each one about every five years!

We were astounded. There was no way the product line could even be explained in a single visit, much less teaching dealer reps how to sell it. And once every five years? What about forgetting? Salespeople turnover? Product line enhancements? Changing sales messages?

The company was also fighting for the reps' mindshare versus competitors, who were in the stores more frequently. The staff may as well have had no training program at all, yet they were perfectly satisfied with it.

The continuing theme throughout this book has been that there is often a disconnect between the fundamental principles of adult learning and the way organizations provide training. As a result, training suffers from the Terrible Too's that keep it from generating payback on business results.

Over the years, we have identified 10 symptoms of dysfunctional organizations that contribute to these types of disconnects.[1] These are factors that you should be on the lookout for as you work to improve your training results.

1. Constant crisis.

With today's business pressures, many organizations have settled into a permanent crisis mode. Management is continually unhappy with performance, everything needs to be done faster and cheaper, peoples' jobs are constantly in jeopardy, nobody is given proper lead time, and so on. It's like everything the organization does is a "rush" job.

As a result, planning takes a back seat. The focus is entirely on short-term results because who knows what the future will bring or if the current team will even survive through the planning timeframe. The effect on the Training department is that it becomes a tactical tool for providing compliance training and for responding to short-term demands for courses.

This is why we've emphasized the need to expand beyond your traditional role as a manufacturer of training and have shown you how to do it. You must become a partner supporting strategic business initiatives and generating one-year payback in excess of your costs.

2. Organizational insanity.

Insanity has been defined as "doing the same thing over and over and expecting a different result." For many Training departments, their version of this seems to be, "If it doesn't work, don't fix it." They do the same old same old and keep asking the classic questions from Part 2 about why people don't take their training and why management doesn't value it.

One way to improve the effectiveness of your training is to work through the relevant To Do lists in the book. These are the "different things" that research shows will generate improved results.

3. Pluralistic ignorance.

It's amazing how many people in organizations don't "get it." When many of them are similarly clueless, then the organization suffers from pluralistic ignorance.

This is when Training departments say things such as:
- "We offer a complete training solution," and a population of 10,000 employees completes only 200 individual programs from a list of thousands.
- "We effectively train our dealer channel," and that means 20 minutes every six months.
- "We teach them everything they need to know at this 2-day meeting," and attendees focus on getting drunk at night.
- "We provide that through e-learning," and students are turning off boring click-and-read programs after 5 minutes.
- "They see that in a webinar," and there is a 60% no-show rate.

When it comes to training, many professionals are fooling themselves. They know learners hate it. Managers don't support it. Yet the message to leadership is that everything is great, all the way until the training budget is axed.

4. Relative success.

It's easy for trainers to fool themselves by comparing their department with those in other, more dysfunctional organizations. ("You think we're bad? You ought to be working for Crack-the-Whip Enterprises.") They make the mistake of looking at relative success rather than absolute success.

Excellence is not relative. It's an absolute. Trainers need to focus on the standards for effective adult learning and measure themselves against that, rather than compare themselves with other organizations that are even less enlightened.

5. Sub-optimizing.

In his seminars, reengineering guru Michael Hammer talked about the problems of fragmented processes.[2] This often results in sub-optimizing (i.e., maximizing a part of the process at the expense of the overall operation).

The problem is illustrated by the singular focus of Training departments on the cost of programs versus the overall results for learners. A Training department can't be successful without making sure the entire training process is executed properly.

6. Indirect causes.

When things aren't going well, an important sign of dysfunction is when the explanations shift to blame impersonal factors instead of root causes. People will say, "Course attendance is down," as if attendance has a will of its own. That feisty attendance—up, down, up, down. Who knows where it's going next? Using this phrasing, no one is ever actually at fault.

Healthy organizations use sentences with cause and effect in them. "Employees dislike the courses" or "The program failed to improve business results." There has to be a *who* and a *what* in there somewhere in order to understand the root cause of an issue. That's the only way you can fix things.

The remaining dysfunctions are aimed more at the overall organization, but we'll quickly cover them here for completeness.

7. OK sorry's.

Dysfunctional organizations can get locked into a "Sorry is OK" mentality. This is not to suggest that being sorry for mistakes is wrong or that blame is even a primary concern. But dysfunctional organizations have a high tolerance for failure, as long as the attitude is right and "lessons have been learned."

Successful organizations focus on preventing problems versus handling them. That's where the real benefits occur.

8. Segmented morals.

Dysfunctional organizations are infected with a flexible morality. Their stated values are often in direct conflict with their actual conduct.

Healthy organizations have a set of values and a behavioral culture that is consistent. Their "do as I say" and "do as I do" formal and informal messages are in agreement.

9. Multi-class society.

Many organizations are heavily segmented by class. Under the guise of "executive productivity," employees are quickly shown who is important and who is not.

In other organizations, even very large ones, all people are viewed as equally valuable. Although there are obvious organizational differences in title, pay, and power, the overall experience is one of a class-free society and culture.

10. Broken behavior consequence chains.

In dysfunctional organizations, people do bad things and nothing bad happens to them. For example, training is not generating any measurable transfer of learning, yet the same learning approach continues unchanged.

In functional organizations, there is a rational action-reward system in operation. It's like the feedback loop in the training process. When people do good things, good things happen to them. When people do bad things, bad things happen to them. People are motivated to achieve because there is a commensurate payoff to be gained.

▷ To Do

Those are the symptoms of a dysfunctional organizational culture that can sidetrack your efforts to improve training.

1. When you see them in an organization, run the other way.

Now What?

YOU HAVE NOW READ 43 CHAPTERS detailing how you can increase the effectiveness of the training you provide. This is your last to-do list.

1. We have no room to point fingers when it comes to cognitive overload. Even chunked up as it is into short chapters, this book is a lot to take in at one time. Read it once and then wait a bit to give it time to sink in.

2. Reread the book. We had to present our concepts in a linear fashion, but they're actually a network of interrelated ideas about effective training. Many of the early chapters will make more sense now that you've read the entire book. You can see where we were going and how the topics support each other.

   Don't feel like you have to review this all at once. The chapters are short. Reread one per day for two months. Or read one per week. (Everyone has 10 minutes per week to learn!)

3. Share this research with your compatriots in the Training department. Then share it with the folks at the big table. Your life will become easier once everyone understands and acknowledges the realities of adult learning.

4. Prioritize. Start thinking about which of the ideas here hold the most potential for you to improve your training offerings.

5. Finally, what is the most important step in the training process? DO IT!

We always closed our classroom programs with this comment: "Everybody wants to learn how to improve themselves, as long as they really don't have to do it."

Make the decision to end any disconnect between your training and the research on effective and efficient learning. Utilize "right" learning techniques in your training and watch your scorecard needles move.

References

▷ Part 1

1. Porter, M.E. & Rivkin, J.W. (2012). Prosperity at Risk: Findings of Harvard Business School's Survey on U.S. Competitiveness. *Harvard Business School.* January: 17.

Chapter 1.1

1. ASTD (2011). *The 2010 ASTD State of the Industry Report.* Alexandria, VA: American Society for Training & Development. January.

2. Adkins, S.S. (2011). *The US Market for Self-paced eLearning Products and Services: 2010-2015 Forecast and Analysis.* Monroe, WA: Ambient Insight. January.

3. Haskell, R.E. (2000). *Transfer of Learning: Cognition and Instruction.* New York: Academic Press.

4. Delahoussaye, M., Ellis, K. & Bolch, M. (2002). Measuring Corporate Smarts. *Training Magazine.* August: 20-35.

5. McMurrer, D., Van Buren, M. & Woodwell, W., Jr. (2000). *The 2000 ASTD State of the Industry Report.* Alexandria, VA: American Society for Training & Development.

6. Clark, D. (n.d.). Learning and Training: Statistics and Myth, http://www.nwlink.com/~donclark/hrd/trainsta.html#elearninggrowth. (accessed October 24, 2011).

Chapter 1.2

1. Thompson, C. (2011). Why Johnny Can't Search. *Wired.* November: 62.

2. Mehrabian, A. (1972). *Silent Messages: Implicit Communication of Emotions and Attitudes.* Florence, KY: Wadsworth Publishing. 75-80.

3. Thalheimer, W. (2006). People remember 10%, 20% … Oh Really? October 8. http://www.willatworklearning.com/2006/10/people_remember.html. (accessed October 24, 2011).

4. Mark, G., Gonzalez, V.M. & Harris, J. (2005). No Task Left Behind? Examining the Nature of Fragmented Work. *CHI Papers.* April 2-7: 321-330.

Chapter 1.3

1. Islam, K. (2010). A Challenge to Training Professionals, October 22, 2010. http://www.trainingindustry.com/blog/blog-entries/a-challenge-to-training-professionals.aspx. (accessed October 25, 2011).

2. Harward, D. (2008). So, You Aren't a CLO—Do You Deserve to Be? February. http://www.cedma-europe.org/newsletter%20articles/TrainingOutsourcing/So,%20 You%20Arent%20a%20CLO%20-%20Do%20You%20Deserve%20to%20Be%20 (Feb%2008).pdf. (accessed October 25, 2011).

◯ Part 2

Chapter 2.3
1. National Institute of Standards (2011). *2011-2012 Criteria for Performance Excellence.* Washington, DC: National Institute of Standards. 51-52.

2. Guaspari, J. & Hay, E. (1993). *TIME: The Next Dimension of Quality.* Video. Watertown, MA: American Management Association.

3. National Institute of Standards.

Chapter 2.4
1. Flandez, R. (2007). Firms Go Online to Train Employees. *The Wall Street Journal.* August 14: B4.

Chapter 2.5
1. Prokopeak, M. (2011). Special Report: Learning Delivery. *Chief Learning Officer.* February 2.

Chapter 2.7
1. Urban Dictionary (n.d.). Pronoid. http://www.urbandictionary.com/define. php?term=pronoid. (accessed November 4, 2011).

◯ Part 3

Chapter 3.1
1. Clark, R., Nguyen, F. & Sweller, J. (2006). *Efficiency in Learning: Evidence-Based Guidelines to Manage Cognitive Load.* San Francisco, CA: Pfeiffer. 143.

2. Paas, F., Renkl, A. & Sweller, J. (2003). Cognitive Load Theory and Instructional Design: Recent Developments. *Educational Psychologist.* 38(1): 104.

Chapter 3.2
1. Clark, R., Nguyen, F. & Sweller, J. (2006). *Efficiency in Learning: Evidence-Based Guidelines to Manage Cognitive Load.* San Francisco, CA: Pfeiffer. 121.

2. Miller G.A. (1956). The magical number seven plus or minus two: some limits on our capacity for processing information. *Psychological Review.* March: 81–97.

3. Baddeley, A. (2000). The episodic buffer: a new component of working memory? *Trends in Cognitive Sciences.* 4(11), November 1: 417-423.

4. Clark, Nguyen & Sweller, 34.

5. Smith, B.D. & Morris, L. (2009). *Breaking Through: College Reading, 9th Ed.* White Plains, NY: Pearson Longman.

6. Clark, R.C. (2008). *Building Expertise: Cognitive Methods for Training and Performance Improvement.* San Francisco, CA: Pfeiffer. 105-107.

Chapter 3.3
1. University of Rochester Medical Center (n.d.). Ability to Concentrate Isn't What It Used to Be. http://webed.miner.rochester.edu/encyclopedia/content.aspx?ContentTypeID=1&ContentID=1140. (accessed November 15, 2011).

2. Carliner, S. (2002). *Designing E-Learning.* Alexandria, VA: American Society of Training and Development. 89.

3. Johnstone, A.H. & Percival, F. (1976). Attention Breaks in Lectures. *Education in Chemistry.* 13(2). March: 49-50.

4. Burns, R.A. (1985). Information impact and factors affecting recall. Paper presented at the Annual National Conference on Teaching Excellence and Conference of Administrators. May.

5. Richardson, H. (2010). Students only have "10-minute attention span." *BBC Mobile News.* January 12.

6. Mark, G., Gonzalez, V.M. & Harris, J. (2005). No Task Left Behind? Examining the Nature of Fragmented Work. *CHI Papers.* April 2-7: 321-330.

7. Lewis, B. (2001). Management skills can save you from becoming a slave to technology. *InfoWorld.* March 5: 42.

Chapter 3.4
1. Ebbinghaus, H. (1913). *Memory: A Contribution to Experimental Psychology.* New York, NY: Columbia University.

2. Cooper, G. & Sweller, J. (1987). Effects of schema acquisition and rule automation on mathematical problem-solving transfer. *Journal of Educational Psychology.* 79(4): 347-362.

3. Ebbinghaus.

Chapter 3.5
1. Clark, R.C. (2008). *Building Expertise: Cognitive Methods for Training and Performance Improvement, 3rd Ed,* San Francisco: Pfeiffer. 285.

◑ Part 4

Chapter 4.1
1. Clark, R., Nguyen, F. & Sweller, J. (2006). *Efficiency in Learning: Evidence-Based Guidelines to Manage Cognitive Load.* San Francisco, CA: Pfeiffer. 267-271.

2. Clark, R.C. (2008). *Building Expertise: Cognitive Methods for Training and Performance Improvement, 3rd Ed,* San Francisco: Pfeiffer. 192.

3. Clark. 100-101.

4. Clark, Nguyen & Sweller. 168-173.

Chapter 4.2
1. Friedenreich, K. & Moine, D.J. (1990). Winning Sales Strategies for the 90's. *Insurance Review,* January: 26-29.

Chapter 4.3
1. Adams, S. (1993). *Dilbert* comic strip. May 4. http://dilbert.com/strips/comic/1993-05-04. (accessed November 29, 2011).

2. National Institute of Standards (2011). *2011-2012 Criteria for Performance Excellence.* Washington, DC: National Institute of Standards. 51-52.

Chapter 4.4
1. Mayer, R.E. (2005). *The Cambridge Handbook of Multimedia Learning.* New York, NY: Cambridge University Press.

2. Garner, R., Gillingham, M. & White, C. (1989). Effects of seductive details on macroprocessing in adults and children. *Cognition and Instruction.* 6(1): 41-57.

3. Clark, R.C. (2008). *Building Expertise: Cognitive Methods for Training and Performance Improvement.* San Francisco, CA: Pfeiffer. 155.

4. Clark, R., Nguyen, F. & Sweller, J. (2006). *Efficiency in Learning: Evidence-Based Guidelines to Manage Cognitive Load.* San Francisco, CA: Pfeiffer. 116.

5. Clark, 39.

Chapter 4.5
1. Virginia Tech (2009). New data from Virginia Tech Transportation Institute provides insight into cell phone use and driving distraction. *Virginia Tech News.* July 29. http://www.vtnews.vt.edu/articles/2009/07/2009-571.html. (accessed December 1, 2011).

2. Mayer, R.E. & Moreno, R. (n.d.). A Cognitive Theory of Multimedia Learning: Implications for Design Principles. Unpublished paper. *University of California–Santa Barbara.* http://www.unm.edu/~moreno/PDFS/chi.pdf. (accessed December 1, 2011). 3.

3. Clark, R.C. (2008). *Building Expertise: Cognitive Methods for Training and Performance Improvement.* San Francisco, CA: Pfeiffer. 129-137.

4. Clark, R.C. & Mayer, R.E., (2008). *e-Learning and the Science of Instruction: Proven Guidelines for Consumers and Designers of Multimedia Learning, 2ⁿᵈ Ed.* San Francisco, CA: Pfeiffer. 77-92.

5. Clark, R., Nguyen, F. & Sweller, J. (2006). *Efficiency in Learning: Evidence-Based Guidelines to Manage Cognitive Load.* San Francisco, CA: Pfeiffer. 77-105.

Chapter 4.6
1. Haidet, P., Morgan, R.O., O'Malley, K., Moran, B.J. & Richards, B.F. (2004). A controlled trial of active versus passive learning strategies in a large group setting. *Advances in Health Sciences Education.* 9: 15-27.

2. Clark, R.C. (2008). *Building Expertise: Cognitive Methods for Training and Performance Improvement.* San Francisco, CA: Pfeiffer. 209.

3. Wetzel, C.D., Radtke, P.H. & Stern, H.W. (1994). *Instructional Effectiveness in Video Media.* Hillsdale: Lawrence Erlbaum Associates. 140.

4. Wilson, B. & Cole, P. (1996). Cognitive Teaching Models. *Handbook of Research for Educational Communications and Technology*, D. Jonassen, Ed. New York: Macmillan. 601-621.

5. Stull, A.T. & Mayer, R.E. (2007). Learning by doing versus learning by viewing: Three experimental comparisons of learner-generated versus author-provided graphic organizers. *Journal of Educational Psychology.* 99:808-820.

6. Mayer, R.E. (2001). *Multimedia Learning.* Cambridge: Cambridge University Press. 19.

7. Marshall, J.M. (2002). Learning with technology: Evidence that technology can, and does, support learning. *Cable in the Classroom.* 7.

Chapter 4.7
1. Clark, R., Nguyen, F. & Sweller, J. (2006). *Efficiency in Learning: Evidence-Based Guidelines to Manage Cognitive Load.* San Francisco, CA: Pfeiffer. 91.

2. Ibid.

3. Clark, R.C. (2008). *Building Expertise: Cognitive Methods for Training and Performance Improvement.* San Francisco, CA: Pfeiffer. 227.

4. Newfields, T. (2000). Creative Note Taking and Study Skills. *Journal of Nanzan Junior College.* 28, December: 59-78.

5. Benton, S.I., Kiewra, K.A., Whitefill, J.M. & Dennison, R. (1993). Encoding and External-Storage Effects on Writing Processes. *Journal of Educational Psychology.* 85(2), June: 267-280.

6. Lane, R. & Kosslyn, S.M. (n.d.). Dump that Text! Transform Your PowerPoint Slides into a Visual Feast. *Microsoft PowerPoint 2007 Help and How-to.* http://office. microsoft.com/en-ca/powerpoint-help/dump-that-text-transform-your-powerpoint-slides-into-a-visual-feast-HA010381809.aspx. (accessed December 2, 2011).

7. Benton, Kiewra, Whitefill & Dennison.

Chapter 4.8

1. Sweller, J. & Cooper, G.A. (1985). The Use of Worked Examples as a Substitute for Problem Solving in Learning Algebra. *Cognition and Instruction.* 21(1):59-89.

2. Atkinson, R.K., Renkl, A. & Merrill, M.M. (2003). Transitioning from Studying Examples to Solving Problems: Effect of Self-Explanation Prompts and Fading Worked Out Steps. *Journal of Educational Psychology.* 95(4): 774-783.

3. Ibid, 775.

4. Ibid, 774-775.

5. Kalyuga, S., Chandler, P. & Sweller, J. (2001). Learner Experience and Efficiency of Instructional Guidance. *Educational Psychology,* 21(1): 5-23.

Chapter 4.9

1. Anderson, L.W. & Torrey, P. (1995). Instructional Pacing. *International Encyclopedia of Teaching and Teacher Education, 2nd Ed. (L.W. Anderson Ed.)* Tarrytown, NY: Elsevier Science.

2. Moreno, R. & Mayer, R.E. (2000). Engaging Students in Active Learning: The Case for Personalized Multimedia Messages. *Journal of Educational Psychology.* 9(4): 724-733.

3. Clark, R.C. & Mayer, R.E., (2008). *e-Learning and the Science of Instruction: Proven Guidelines for Consumers and Designers of Multimedia Learning, 2nd Ed.* San Francisco, CA: Pfeiffer. 138-139.

4. Ibid, 144.

5. Ibid, 148.

6. Ibid, 79.

7. Neiderhauser, D.S., Reynolds, R.E., Salmen, D.J. & Skolmoski, P. (2000). The Influence of Cognitive Load on Learning from Hypertext. *Journal of Educational Computer Research.* 23(3): 237-255.

8. National Research Council (1991). *In the Mind's Eye: Enhancing Human Performance, D. Druckman & R.A. Bjork (Eds.)* Washington, DC: National Academy Press. 30.

9. Clark & Mayer, 236-242.

10. Dixon, N.M. (1990). The Relationship between Trainee Responses on Participant Reaction Forms and Posttest Scores. *Human Resource Development Quarterly*. 1(2), Summer: 129-137.

▷ Part 5

Chapter 5.1

1. Prokopeak, M. (2011). Special Report: Learning Delivery. *Chief Learning Officer*. February 2.

2. Adams, G.L. (1992). Why Interactive? *Multimedia & Videodisc Monitor*. March.

3. Shachar, M. & Neuman, Y. (2003). Differences Between Traditional and Distance Education Academic Performances: A meta-analytic approach. *International Review of Research in Open and Distance Learning*. (4)2, October: 13.

4. Means, B., Toyama, Y., Murphy, R., Bakia, M. & Jones, K. (2009). *Evaluation of Evidence-Based Practices in Online Learning: A Meta-Analysis and Review of Online Learning Studies*. Washington, DC: U.S. Department of Education. ix.

5. SR Education Group (n.d.). Guide to Online Schools. http://www.guidetoonlin-eschools.com. (accessed December 6, 2011).

6. OnLineHighSchool.org (n.d.). Tuition Free Online High Schools. http://www.onlinehighschool.org/Free_Online_High_Schools.html. (accessed December 6, 2011).

7. Brandon Hall (1997). *Web-Based Training Cookbook*. Hoboken, NJ: Wiley. 108.

Chapter 5.3

1. Kapp, K. (2007). Today's Toys, Tomorrow's Tools. *Training Day*. March 31. http://vnutravel.typepad.com/trainingday/2007/03/todays_toys_tom.html. (accessed December 6, 2011).

2. Lee, J.E. (2008). 2008 Learning & Talent Management Technology Survey Results. Knowledge Management Solutions. White paper. July 7. http://www.kmsi.us/white_paper11.htm. (accessed December 15, 2008).

Chapter 5.4

1. Masie, E. (2011). Webinar No-Show Rates? *Learning Trends*. No. 680: August 30.

2. Cooper, K. (1979). *BodyBusiness: The Sender's and Receiver's Guide to Nonverbal Communication*. New York, NY: AMACOM. 162-178.

Chapter 5.5

1. Gerlach, J.M. (1994). Is This Colaboration? *Collaborative Learning: Underlying Processes and Effective Techniques, Bosworth K. & Hamilton, S.J. Eds*. San Francisco, CA: Jossey-Bass Publishers. Fall No. 59: 5-14.

2. Hart, J. (n.d.). The Future of E-Learning is Social Learning. http://www.slideshare.net/janehart/the-future-of-elearning-is-social-learnng. (accessed December 9, 2011).

3. Spira, J.B. & Goldes, D.M. (2007). *Information Overload: We Have Met the Enemy and He Is Us.* New York, NY: Basex. February: 10.

Chapter 5.6
1. Entertainment Software Association (2011). *Essential Facts About the Computer and Video Game Industry.* Washington, DC: Entertainment Software Association.

2. Cross, T. (2011). All the World's a Game. *The Economist.* December 10, 2011.

3. Ritke-Jones, W. (2010). *Virtual Environments for Corporate Education: Employee Learning and Solutions.* Hershey, PA: Business Science Reference. 114-120.

4. Bell, B.S., Kanar, A.M. & Kozlowski, S.W.J. (2008). Current Issues and Future Directions in Simulation-Based Training in North America. *The International Journal of Human Resource Management, 19(8).* January 1: 1416-1434.

5. Jacobs, R.L. & Baum, M. (1987). Simulation and Games in Training and Development: Status and Concerns about Their Use. *Simulation & Games,* 18(3), September: 385-394.

6. Chapman, B. (2004). *E-Learning Simulation Products and Services.* Del Ray Beach, FL: Brandon Hall.

Chapter 5.7
1. Hampel, P. (2011). Pay phones fading away. *St. Louis Post-Dispatch.* December 11: C1-C4.

2. Quesinberry, N. (2011). Why Mobile Learning? *JPL Integrated Communications.* October 31. http://learningsolutions.jplcreative.com/blog/index.php/2011/10/31/why-mobile-learning. (accessed December 15, 2011).

3. Udell, C. (2011). Dear Companies, You Should Start Using Mobile Devices as Training Tools for Your Employees. *Business Insider.* November 8. http://articles.businessinsider.com/2011-11-08/strategy/30372370_1_smartphones-employees-devices. (accessed December 15, 2011).

4. Hardy, E. (2010). Google Adopts a New Strategy: Mobile First. *Brighthand Smartphone News & Reviews.* February 17. http://www.brighthand.com/default.asp?newsID=16235&news=Google+Android+OS+CEO+Eric+Schmidt+Mobile+First. (accessed December 15, 2011).

Chapter 5.8
1. Creswell, J. (2009). How to Start a Company (and Kiss Like Angelina). *New York Times,* July 11.

2. Saltrick, S., Honey, M. & Pasnik, S. (2004). *Television Goes to School: The impact of television on formal learning.* Washington, DC: Corporation for Public Broadcasting. June: 4.

3. Schadler, T., with Brown, M. & Burnes, S. (2009). Tap the Potential of "YouTube for the Enterprise." *Forrester Research.* January 17.

4. Choi, J.C. & Johnson, S.D. (2005). The Effect of Context-Based Video Instruction on Learning and Motivation in Online Courses. *American Journal of Distance Education.* 19(4). December: 215-227.

5. Musich, P. (2007). Cisco charts new course. *eWeek.* January 7: 56-59.

6. Masie, E. (2010). Learning Trends. *The Masie Center.* Newsletter. March 2.

7. ___ (2011). Learning Trends. *The Masie Center.* Newsletter. January 5.

8. Semuels, A. (2009). Television viewing at all-time high. *The Los Angeles Times.* February 24.

9. Clark, R.C. & Mayer, R.E., (2008). *e-Learning and the Science of Instruction: Proven Guidelines for Consumers and Designers of Multimedia Learning, 2nd Ed.* San Francisco, CA: Pfeiffer. 167-178.

Part 6

Chapter 6.1
1. Haskell, R.E. (2000). *Transfer of Learning: Cognition, instruction, and reasoning.* New York, NY: Academic Press. 5.

2. Bunch, K. J. (2007). Training Failure as a Consequence of Organizational Culture. *Human Resource Development Review.* 6(2), June: 142.

3. Brinkerhoff, R.O. (2008). Training Impact Evaluation That Senior Leaders Believe and Use: The Success Case Method. Workshop presented at Training 2008 Exposition and Conference, Atlanta, GA. February 4.

4. Peterson, B. (2004). Unpublished paper from Apollo Consulting Group. University of Phoenix.

5. Bersin, J. (2009). Informal Learning becomes Formal. *Bersin & Associates.* January 22. http://www.bersin.com/blog/post/Informal-Learning-becomes-Formal.aspx. (accessed November 17, 2011).

6. Kirkpatrick, J.D. & Kirkpatrick, W.K. (2010). *Training on Trial: How Workplace Learning Must Reinvent Itself to Remain Relevant.* New York, NY: AMACOM. 7.

7. Ibid.

8. Peterson.

Chapter 6.2
1. Marx, A. (n.d.). The AIM Process. *AIM Consulting.* http://aim-consult.com/process.htm. (accessed January 20, 2012).

2. Clark, R.C. (2008). *Building Expertise: Cognitive Methods for Training and Performance Improvement, 3rd Ed,* San Francisco: Pfeiffer. 238-239.

Chapter 6.4
1. Cullen, L.T. (2007). Employee Diversity Training Doesn't Work. *Time.* April 26.

◗ Part 7
Chapter 7.1
1. YouTube (n.d.). Press Room: Statistics. http://www.youtube.com/t/press_statistics. (accessed December 29, 2011).

Chapter 7.2
1. Piktialis, D. & Greenes, K.A. (2008). *Bridging the Gaps: How to Transfer Knowledge in Today's Multigenerational Workplace.* The Conference Board Research Report. R-1428-08-RR, July: 4.

2. Vappie, K. (2009). *The Business Case for Mentoring.* Burlington, ME: Linkage. 4.

3. Haaga, J. (2002). Just How Many Baby Boomers Are There? *Population Reference Bureau.* December. http://www.prb.org/Articles/2002/JustHowManyBabyBoomers AreThere.aspx. (accessed December 28, 2011).

4. Pew Research Center (2011). 10,000 Baby Boomers Retire. *The Databank.* December 28. http://pewresearch.org/databank/dailynumber/?NumberID=1150. (accessed December 28, 2011).

5. Vappie, 4.

6. Stein, N. (2000). Winning the War to Keep Top Talent. *Fortune.* May 29.

Chapter 7.4
1. Cooper, K. (1998). Symptoms of the Dysfunctional Organization. *CooperComm Briefings,* October.

2. Hammer, M. & Champy, J. (1993). *Reengineering the Corporation: A Manifesto for Business Revolution.* New York, NY: HarperBusiness. 28-29.

Index

About the Authors

DAN COOPER is a founding partner and CEO of Performance Improvement Results, a technology-based content development, delivery, and consulting provider headquartered in Kansas City. He has developed hundreds of computer-based and video training programs, and is a member of the Institute for Human Resources Technology Enabled Learning advisory board (HR.com).

Dan was recognized in 2011 by *Training Magazine* as a "Top Young Trainer" and has served on its editorial board. He also has produced a monthly "Video 4 Results" video series for TrainingMag.com and has written a monthly training column for the site.

KEN COOPER is a founding partner of Performance Improvement Results. He has over 30 years of experience as a training consultant and speaker, has presented over 2,500 seminars, and has appeared in hundreds of live and recorded e-learning programs.

Ken is author of *The Relational Enterprise, Effective Competency Modeling and Reporting,* and *BodyBusiness*, all from the American Management Association. He has written hundreds of articles and white papers, and he has been published in *Chief Learning Officer, Training, Trainer's Workshop, The Corporate Board*, and numerous other business publications.

www.piresults.com